CRYPTO DICTIONARY

CRYPTO DICTIONARY

500 Tasty Tidbits for the Curious Cryptographer

by Jean-Philippe Aumasson

**no starch
press**

San Francisco

CRYPTO DICTIONARY. Copyright © 2021 by Jean-Philippe Aumasson

Printed in the United States of America

First printing

25 24 23 22 21   1 2 3 4 5 6 7 8 9

ISBN-13: 978-1-7185-0140-9 (print)
ISBN-13: 978-1-7185-0141-6 (ebook)

Publisher: William Pollock
Execuitve Editor: Barbara Yien
Production Editor: Paula Williamson
Developmental Editors: Frances Saux and Athabasca Witschi
Cover Illustration: Rick Reese
Interior Design and Composition: Maureen Forys, Happenstance Type-O-Rama
Technical Reviewer: Pascal Junod
Copyeditor: Anne Marie Walker
Proofreader: James Fraleigh

For information on book distributors or translations, please contact No Starch Press, Inc. directly:
No Starch Press, Inc.
245 8th Street, San Francisco, CA 94103
phone: 1-415-863-9900; info@nostarch.com
www.nostarch.com

The Library of Congress Control Number is: 2020946022

À Melina

About the Author

Jean-Philippe (JP) Aumasson is the Chief Security Officer and cofounder of Taurus Group, a Swiss financial tech company specializing in digital assets infrastructure. Since 2006, he has authored more than 60 research articles in the field of cryptography and designed the widely used cryptographic algorithms BLAKE2 and SipHash. The author of the acclaimed book *Serious Cryptography* (No Starch Press, 2017), he speaks regularly at information security and technology conferences.

About the Technical Reviewer

Pascal Junod has worked in applied (and less applied) cryptography for a living since 1999, both in the academic and industrial worlds. He holds a master's in computer science from ETH Zurich and a PhD in cryptography from EPF Lausanne. In his spare time, he loves trail running, white-water kayaking, reading books, and caring about his family.

PREFACE

I promise nothing complete; because any human thing
supposed to be complete must for that very reason infallibly
be faulty. I shall not pretend to a minute anatomical
description of the various species, or—in this space at least—
to much of any description. My object here is simply to
project the draught of a systematization of cetology.
I am the architect, not the builder.

—**HERMAN MELVILLE,** in *Moby Dick* (Chapter XXXII)

Crypto Dictionary is quite different from my previous book. Its format and lighter tone might make it look less serious, but its seriousness lies in its breadth of treatment. Whereas *Serious Cryptography* covered applied crypto's fundamentals, or less than 10 percent of all there is to know in the field, this dictionary has the pretension of covering at least 75 percent of cryptography's realm.

The unhurried, gradual, and relatively deep exposition in *Serious Cryptography* is replaced with a less headache-inducing structure filled with concise, direct definitions. This coffee-table book form intends to expose the richness of cryptography, including its exotic and underappreciated corners, to share knowledge and be a gateway to a better appreciation of the science of secrecy.

As the epigraph hints, *Crypto Dictionary* isn't an attempt to deliver a real dictionary that would comprehensively and consistently cover cryptography's diverse areas. You might not find your favorite protocol or cipher and will probably be surprised by the absence of certain terms that I purposefully omitted or just didn't think of. But you'll find many of the major notions and algorithms that cryptographers encounter today, as well as an opinionated selection of terms that I found of practical, theoretical, historical, or anecdotal interest.

Seasoned cryptographers might observe that the book isn't very egalitarian. Although I attempted to cover all streets and alleys of cryptography evenly, certain neighborhoods are inevitably more equally treated than others due to my biases, experience, interests, and variable inspiration. I hope this heterogeneity won't be perceived as unfairness, because that was definitely not my intention.

For example, I chose not to list individuals or software components; instead, the book focuses on the concepts and cryptographic objects that people created and that engineers implemented, which I believe are of greater interest. In accordance with the no-software rule, I didn't include the Signal application, yet I did include the Signal protocol. But this rule suffered one exception, which you'll find between the letters *N* and *P*.

This dictionary doesn't pretend to provide a precise description of the various protocols, algorithms, and other cryptologic notions. *Crypto Dictionary* isn't an encyclopedia and doesn't aim to be a modern version of the venerable *Handbook of Applied Cryptography*. Readers who seek, for example, a formal definition of attribute-based cryptography or a detailed specification of AES will find plenty of references online.

Most definitions are actual definitions, but they vary in how informative they are. I didn't strive for a consistent level of detail and deliberately just minimally explained certain terms—including some of the most established ones—or only added some humorous comment.

Crypto in *Crypto Dictionary* represents cryptography in its most general sense, encompassing the supposed unholy territory of cryptocurrency. But admittedly, the dictionary is far from being a blockchain dictionary, because many of the terms specific to blockchain applications are omitted.

Crypto Dictionary was written to be an entertaining read for everyone, from high school students and novice engineers to PhDs and retired researchers. The goal is that any reader can open the book at a random page and discover a yet unknown notion, excavate an obscure concept, or read an anecdote about a familiar term. Because modern cryptography is such a broad field, it's impossible, even for professional practitioners and researchers, to be familiar with all its notions, let alone master them. For example, who will already be familiar with CECPQ, EKMS, fuzzy extractors, *and* the MASH hash function?

One of the initial motivations was to create a book that would briefly describe nontrivial cryptography concepts, including established ones, as well as some of the most recent research. Many cryptographers have heard these terms but routinely fail to remember what they're about or how they differ from related notions. For example, what is the difference between group signatures and ring signatures? Between a SNARK and a STARK? Between SRP and OPAQUE? Between BIKE and SIKE? What are laconic proofs, puncturable encryption, or verifiable delay functions? Few other books will mention any of these concepts, and most likely, no other will mention all of them.

I would like to issue multiple editions with updates and new definitions listed based on research's progress. Therefore, I want to keep this book alive and make it a bit less incomplete as the years pass, which will require help from you, its readers. I encourage you to share any comment, error report, or additional suggestion by writing to the @cryptolexicon Twitter account (preferably publicly, but as a private DM if you want).

I hope this book will be a pleasurable and valuable read, that it will help you appreciate the richness of the cryptographic landscape, and that, even if cryptography is a very serious topic, you won't take it too seriously.

Lausanne, January 2021

ACKNOWLEDGMENTS

You might be tempted to think that this book is just the fruit of my erudition, but nothing could be further from the truth. Not only did I have to learn or rediscover many of the terms defined in the book, I also relied on peers and specialists to answer questions, review definitions for correctness and clarity, provide me with references, suggest additional definitions, and offer other valuable advice.

I'm particularly indebted to the technical reviewer, Pascal Junod, who spotted numerous inaccuracies in the initial draft and identified important missing definitions. Special thanks also go to Luca De Feo for his review and help with explaining isogenies and hyperelliptic curves in simple terms. I also want to thank Alon Rosen, Anastasiia Voitova, Arrigo Triulzi, Ben Fuller, Doug Henkins, Jason Donenfeld, Nadim Kobeissi, Samuel Neves, and Sofía Celi for their help. Last but not least, I'm grateful to the No Starch team for their support, quality editing, and general professionalism.

CRYPTO DICTIONARY

2013

The year of Edward Snowden's leaks about the NSA's classified activities, a turning point in cryptography. End-to-end encryption suddenly becomes an appealing topic.

65537

The most common RSA public exponent; large enough to not be insecure, small enough to make exponentiation fast, and of a form that optimizes implementations' speed ($65537 = 2^{16} + 1$).

A5/0

One of the three encryption modes in early mobile telephony standards (GSM). A5/0 just means *no encryption*; therefore, the audio content from a mobile call would be received and transmitted in the clear between a mobile device and the nearest base station. It's as secure as early TLS versions' *null cipher*.

A5/1

The default GSM cipher in Western countries (prior to 3G and 4G technologies) that encrypts encoded audio mobile communications. A stream cipher based on a curious mechanism involving three linear feedback shift registers irregularly clocked; so the update of a register depends on the values of certain bits in the two other registers. Sophisticated cryptanalytic attacks have broken A5/1. But in practice, the most effective attack is relatively simple: it's a time-memory trade-off that exploits the short state of A5/1 (64 bits) and involves the precomputation of large rainbow tables. The A5/1 specification was initially confidential and unavailable to the public until it was reverse engineered in the late 1990s.

A5/2

The export version of A5/1, a euphemism meaning its technical requirements include something like *must be easy to break by Western nations' intelligence agencies.* Designed to be insecure, A5/2 didn't turn out to be outrageously insecure: after being reverse engineered around the same time as A5/1, academic researchers quickly found attacks on A5/2. But these attacks were more efficient on paper than in practice.

A5/3

At last, a real cipher in mobile phones. An upgrade to the do-it-yourself A5/1 that applies an algorithm already public and vetted, namely the block cipher KASUMI. KASUMI was used in 2G (along with A5/1), in 3G as A5/4 (along with SNOW 3G), and was no longer supported in 4G.

🔓 See *KASUMI.*

A5/4

A5/3 but with a key of 128 bits instead of 64 bits; A5/4 is secure, whereas A5/3 isn't.

Adaptive attack

An attack in which the attacker's actions depend on what they observe during the attack and the protocol's execution. For example, in an adaptive chosen-plaintext attack, the attacker sends plaintext messages that depend on the responses to their previous queries. In a nonadaptive attack, the list of plaintexts for which the attacker queries the ciphertexts must be predetermined.

AEAD (authenticated encryption with associated data)

A type of symmetric cipher that encrypts and authenticates data by producing a ciphertext as well as an authentication tag. The decryption step then only succeeds if the tag is valid, which proves that the ciphertext was created by someone who knows the key. To validate the tag, the receiving end generally computes it from the encrypted message and verifies that the computed value is identical to the one received.

The AD in AEAD refers to associated data—also called *additional* or *auxiliary*— or data that isn't encrypted but is covered by the authentication mechanism, because it's taken as an input when computing the authentication tag.

AEAD can be realized in three ways:

- With an established cipher and established MAC, such as AES in CBC mode as a cipher and HMAC-SHA-256 as a MAC. This is the traditional approach that is usually the least efficient. It's also the most error prone because of the different ways to combine a cipher and a MAC (so-called encrypt-and-MAC, encrypt-then-MAC, and MAC-then-encrypt.

- With an established cipher and ad hoc MAC or mode, such as AES-GCM and ChaCha20-Poly1305, which are currently the most popular AEADs of this type. For example, TLS 1.3. AES-SIV also belongs in this category, although it's a bit different (a MAC-and-encrypt rather than encrypt-then-MAC construction).

- With a custom 2-in-1 construction, such as ACORN and AEGIS, both ciphers selected by the CAESAR competition. In these algorithms, the same internal state and logic encrypts and generates the authentication tag.

AES (Advanced Encryption Standard)

The ubiquitous block cipher standardized by NIST in 2000. Designed by Belgian cryptographers Joan Daemen and Vincent Rijmen, and winner of the AES competition, its use is universal today under its various modes of operation, such as CBC, GCM, and SIV.

🔓 See *Rijndael.*

AES-CCM

AES in counter-with-CBC-MAC mode, which combines the CTR encryption mode with CBC-MAC authentication. AES-CCM is a NIST standard and is supported in TLS 1.3 and several other protocols, including Bluetooth Low Energy. But it's much less popular than its sibling AES-GCM. The reason is that AES-CCM is generally slower and less convenient to use than AES-GCM. A research paper titled "A Critique of CCM" describes the limitations of the CCM mode.

AES-CCM sometimes fits better than AES-GCM in embedded platforms because it only needs an AES algorithm and no additional logic (unlike GCM's GMAC).

AES-GCM

AES in Galois counter mode, the most common authenticated encryption primitive at the time of writing. Also the primitive that ended the reign of HMAC authenticators. In GCM mode, a message is encrypted in CTR mode and the Galois MAC (GMAC, aka GHASH) generates an authentication tag from the ciphertext and associated data blocks. The carry-less multiplication instruction PCLMULQDQ was introduced in Intel CPUs in the 2010s to speed up GMAC computations.

AES-GCM'S ACHILLES' HEEL

AES-GCM is secure except when called twice with the same nonce on distinct messages, which can leak plaintext data and reveal the authentication key GMAC uses. This unfortunate fragility hasn't stopped AES-GCM from being used in countless protocols (including TLS, IPSec, and SSH) and from being standardized by IEEE, ISO, and NIST. AES-GCM's cousin AES-GCM-SIV eliminates the nonce-reuse problem but isn't yet widely supported and is a bit slower.

AES-GCM-SIV

A variant of AES-GCM where the encryption nonce is determined from the tag computed by authenticating the plaintext (and any associated data). AES-GCM-SIV's MAC, called *POLYVAL*, is slightly different from GCM's GMAC: whereas AES-GCM is of the encrypt-then-MAC form, AES-GCM-SIV is a MAC-and-encrypt construction. The main benefit of AES-GCM-SIV compared to AES-GCM is that the former remains secure if a same nonce is reused—a property called *misuse resistance*.

AES-NI

Officially AES New Instructions but often called native instructions, which might be a better term. AES-NIs are CPU instructions that compute AES using hardware logic in the chip's silicon as opposed to a combination of arithmetic operations using the chip's ALU. When introduced by Intel in 2008, AES-NIs made AES software about 10 times faster, and as a by-product, immune to cache-timing attacks.

AES-SIV

🔒 See *SIV-AES*.

AIM (Advanced INFOSEC Machine)

A chipset designed by Motorola in the late 1990s that includes separate FPGAs for red and black operations. Pompously advertised as *one of the most revolutionary advances in cryptography, ever.* The NSA uses it to protect classified and sensitive national security information. The off-the-shelf AIM didn't include classified (Suite A) algorithms, but users could program the FPGAs to support algorithms, such as ACCORDION or BATON.

AKA

In 3GPP standards parlance, the authenticated key agreement operation between users of a cellular network and the user's home network, which might be different from the serving network.

AKA IN 3GPP STANDARDS

The AKA is very similar in 3G UMTS, 4G LTE, and 5G standards, and unlike many other key agreement protocols doesn't use public key primitives; instead, it relies on a shared symmetric key and pseudorandom functions (except in 5G where public-key encryption is added).

The AKA looks like a straightforward protocol, taking a master key and a sequence number to derive session keys (encryption, authentication, and anonymity keys) while ensuring mutual authentication, or more precisely mutual knowledge of the shared key. But despite its cryptographic boringness, AKA aims to achieve other, nontrivial goals specific to its unique environment. These goals include confidentiality of the user identity (IMSI), unlinkability of the user, authentication of the serving network (by the user and home network), and strong unreliability guarantees and resilience to unsafe pseudorandom generators.

AKS (Agrawal-Kayal-Saxena)

The first deterministic primality test, as opposed to randomized ones. The 2002 research paper presenting the AKS algorithm, "PRIMES is in P," was the first proof that the problem of primality testing is in the P complexity class, or the class of problems for which a nonrandomized polynomial-time algorithm exists.

🔓 See *PRIMES*.

Algebraic cryptanalysis

A form of cryptanalysis where the target problem (typically key recovery, but also forgery, distinguishing, and so on) is modeled as a system of multivariate equations to which a solution is found by generic or ad hoc techniques. Algebraic cryptanalysis has been used to attack symmetric and asymmetric cryptosystems. An example target is stream ciphers based on feedback shift registers with low algebraic degree logic, giving rise to underlying equations exploitable by algebraic attacks.

🔓 See *Gröbner basis*.

Alice

Bob's partner in crime, but who never met Bob in person. According to their official biography in John Gordon's 1984 speech: "Alice and Bob have tried to defraud insurance companies, they've played poker for high stakes by mail, and they've exchanged secret messages over tapped telephones. (. . .) Alice and Bob have very powerful enemies. One of their enemies is the Tax Authority. Another is the Secret Police. This is a pity, since their favorite topics of discussion are tax frauds and overthrowing the government."

🔓 See *Bob*.

All-or-nothing transform (AONT)

A reversible transformation where you need every bit of the output to determine any bit of the input. When an encryption scheme is an AONT, the decryption key is useless to determine the plaintext if you miss some bits of the ciphertext (unless the missing bits are so few that they can be brute-forced). The OAEP construction used for RSA encryption is an example of AONT. CBC or GCM encryption modes aren't AONTs.

Anonymous signature

A signature that doesn't reveal the identity (public key) of the signer and therefore needs some interaction with the signer to verify it. It implies invisibility.

🔒 See *Invisible signature.*

Applied Cryptography

The 1996 book by Bruce Schneier that has been the main reference in the field for many years; it introduced many students and engineers to cryptography. Famous for its opening paragraph: "There are two kinds of cryptography in this world: cryptography that will stop your kid sister from reading your files, and cryptography that will stop major governments from reading your files. This book is about the latter."

Inevitably outdated 25 years after its publication, *Applied Cryptography* is still worth keeping on your shelf as long as you don't blindly follow all of its recommendations. It's also much less outdated than Schneier's two prior books, *E-Mail Security* and *Protect Your Macintosh*.

Applied cryptography

The part of cryptography that emphasizes direct applications. In contrast, theoretical cryptography is less about engineering and more about fundamental understanding and analysis. The term *applied* is deceiving; both applied and theoretical cryptography can (and ought to?) be equally relevant to real applications.

ARC4

The original name of the RC4 stream cipher; also written as ARCFOUR. Before the reverse engineered RC4 was confirmed to be the actual RC4, it was prudently referred to as *alleged RC4*, which was shortened to ARC4.

Argon2

A password hashing function developed during the Password Hashing Competition. Also, a de facto standard for processing passwords or any low-entropy secret to derive cryptographic keys or store a verifier in a way that prevents efficient cracking using GPUs, FPGAs, dedicated hardware, precomputed tables, or side-channel attacks.

Unlike PBKDF2, Argon2 can enforce the use of a certain amount of memory in addition to a configurable number of iterations. Unlike bcrypt, this amount of memory can be an arbitrary value rather than fixed. Unlike scrypt and the two others, Argon2 offers a user-friendly interface to easily pick time and memory parameters. It's also a simple design that only uses the hash function BLAKE2 internally rather than a combination of all the cryptography ever designed.

🔒 See *bcrypt, scrypt, PBKDF2 (Password-Based Key Derivation Function 2)*.

ARX (Add-Rotate-XOR)

An abbreviation that denotes cryptographic algorithms only doing integer additions, word bit shifts or rotations, and XORs (as opposed to, for example, algorithms using S-boxes). It was coined by cryptography and security researcher Ralf-Philipp Weinmann in 2009.

ASIACRYPT

Asia's top academic cryptography conference, held every autumn in a different location in the Asia-Pacific region since 1990. The only IACR conference that includes *IACR* as a substring of its name. Researchers present peer-reviewed research papers with titles such as "Structure-Preserving and Re-Randomizable RCCA-Secure Public Key Encryption and Its Applications" and "Cryptanalysis of GSM Encryption in 2G/3G Networks Without Rainbow Tables."

🔒 See *CHES, CRYPTO, Eurocrypt, FSE, PKC, Real World Crypto, TCC*.

Asymmetric cryptography

🔒 See *Public-key cryptography*.

Attack

In the context of cryptanalysis, the demonstration of a technique, described as an algorithm, that violates a security claim made by the designers of the primitive or protocol attacked.

NOT ALL ATTACKS ARE ATTACKS

If Alice designs a cipher, she could claim that nobody can 1) recover the secret key with certainty if 2) they're given a list of one billion pairs of plaintext or ciphertext. Here, point 1 is the security goal and point 2 is the attacker model. So if you determine how to recover the key with certainty with one million plaintext or ciphertext pairs, it qualifies as an attack. If you need 10 billion pairs, it doesn't qualify as an attack. If the chance to recover the key is only 1/10, it doesn't qualify either.

The existence of an attack doesn't necessarily imply that the attacked primitive isn't safe to use. For example, if an attack works in 2^{200} operations and the security claim was 2^{256}, you don't have to worry because in reality 2^{200} is as practically impossible as 2^{256}.

Researchers often present attacks in the form of a research paper. When the attack is feasible, an actual implementation might be provided as evidence that it works.

Attribute-based encryption (ABE)

A generalization of identity-based encryption from one attribute (the identity) to more than one. It allows you to encrypt a message not to a given recipient, but to a set of attributes in such a way that only parties satisfying a valid combination of attributes can decrypt the message.

ABE sounds powerful but hasn't found many real applications. Allegedly, the reason is due to its relatively complex construction (using elliptic-curve pairings) and the need for a trusted third party (holding the master key needed to generate private keys).

🔒 See *Identity-based encryption.*

ABE FOR ACCESS CONTROL

ABE is sometimes pitched as suitable for fine-grained access control. For example, you can imagine an organization deploying ABE to encrypt sensitive documents by using attributes such as department, clearance level, and project to cryptographically enforce multilevel security and role-based access. For instance, a document might be encrypted by using a public key with the attributes {department=ENGINEERING, clearance=SECRET, project=LABRADOR}.

ABE could then guarantee that if you satisfy only two of these attributes (say, your department is ENGINEERING and your clearance is SECRET but you work on the project HUSKY), you won't be able to decrypt the document. More interestingly, ABE guarantees that you won't be able to decrypt the document by colluding with someone on the project LABRADOR in the ENGINEERING department if they only have CONFIDENTIAL clearance.

Authenticated cipher

🔒 See *AEAD*.

Axolotl

The original name of the Signal application's end-to-end messaging protocol.

🔒 See *Signal protocol*.

Backdoor

A covert feature to bypass an algorithm or protocol's security. Trapdoors are known by users to exist; backdoors usually are not. A backdoor was once defined as *a feature or defect that allows surreptitious access to data*. A good backdoor must be undetectable, NOBUS (no-one-but-us, or exclusively exploitable by its architects), reusable, unmodifiable, and deniable.

For these reasons, backdoors in cryptographic algorithms are difficult to design and are more easily added in implementations, especially when the internal logic isn't open and hard to deobfuscate. The NSA backdoor in Dual_EC_DRBG is a notable exception. Unfortunately, the most interesting research about backdoors isn't presented at IACR conferences.

Backtracking resistance

Term notably used by NIST to refer to a notion similar to forward secrecy. The opposite of prediction resistance.

🔒 See *Forward secrecy*.

Backward secrecy

The opposite of forward secrecy: backward secrecy is the property that if an attacker compromises some secret values, future messages remain protected. If an entire system's state is compromised— including long-term and short-term keys as well as any secret state or counter—backward secrecy is often impossible. An exception is pseudo-random generators, where uncertainty can be brought into the system via reseeding from reliable entropy sources, preventing an attacker from determining future output bits from a past snapshot of the system. In the context of secure messaging, some models assume that an attacker would compromise only certain sets of keys, but not necessarily the entire local secret state: in this case, some form of backward secrecy might be guaranteed.

🔓 See *Forward secrecy*.

BACKWARD SECRECIES

Often defined in an ad hoc manner, the concept of backward secrecy also appeared under the terms *post-compromise security* (in the context of secure messaging), *break-in recovery* (Signal protocol), *future secrecy* (Signal protocol), *healing* (ZRTP), and *prediction resistance* (NIST).

Base64

Not encryption.

BassOmatic

A cipher initially designed by Phil Zimmermann, the creator of PGP, to encrypt data in PGP. It was found to be insecure and replaced by IDEA in 1991. As Zimmermann commented in the source code, "BassOmatic gets its name from an old Dan Aykroyd *Saturday Night Live* skit involving a blender and a whole fish. The BassOmatic algorithm does to data what the original BassOmatic did to the fish."

BB84

The first quantum key distribution (QKD) construction. It was described by Bennett and Brassard in 1984 and was based on ideas from the concept of quantum money, introduced a year earlier.

bcrypt

A hash algorithm: it doesn't encrypt. Defined to address the obsolescence of the 1976 crypt utility in the 1999 paper "A Future-Adaptable

Password Scheme." In this paper, the authors made the following prediction: "Failing a major breakthrough in complexity theory, these algorithms should allow password-based systems to adapt to hardware improvements and remain secure 20 years into the future."

You can argue that this prophecy was accurate, because you can tune bcrypt to be slow enough to defeat password cracking. On the other hand, bcrypt's 4KB memory usage is now too low to prevent efficient cracking.

Biclique cryptanalysis

An attack against cryptographic algorithms that works by searching for bicliques. In graph theory, a clique is a subset of nodes that are all connected to each other. A biclique is composed of two subsets of nodes; each node from the first subset is connected to all nodes from the second.

This concept was applied to refine differential attacks on AES and lead to attacks that, in theory, perform fewer operations than a brute-force search (2^{126} instead of 2^{127}). The bicliques used in this context are composed of a first set of bits from the internal state, a second set of bits from the ciphertext, and dependencies between these two sets conditioned by key bits. The idea of the attack is then to identify certain bits of the key as those for which the biclique conditions are satisfied (in terms of XOR differences).

BIKE (Bit Flipping Key Encapsulation)

Sounds like SIKE: also a KEM; also post-quantum, but based on a decoding problem rather than an isogeny problem.

🔒 See *SIKE (Supersingular Isogeny Key Encapsulation)*.

BIP (Bitcoin improvement proposal)

A misleading name, because the most famous BIPs are no longer just proposals but de facto standards that apply to more cryptocurrencies than just Bitcoin. These BIPs include:

⚷ BIP 32, which defines a tree-based mechanism to derive key pairs and addresses from a secret seed to create wallets of multiple accounts from a single secret value.

- BIP 44, which assigns semantics to BIP 32 tree levels and defines a syntax for paths within this tree (consisting of purpose, coin type, account, address type, and address index).

- BIP 39, which defines a representation of a secret value as a high-entropy list of dictionary words, or mnemonic, which is then hashed to a seed that will be the root of a BIP 32 hierarchy of accounts.

Bit Gold

The closest predecessor of Bitcoin.

Bitcoin

An experiment that went out of control, for better or for worse.

Black

NSA jargon referring to encrypted values. A black key is an encrypted key that uses, for example, a key wrapping mechanism so that it can be safely distributed on lower-security-level systems or networks. In the context of data-at-rest protection, black data is classified data that has been encrypted twice using appropriate encryption layers.

🔒 See *EKMS (Electronic Key Management System)*.

BLAKE

A hash function submitted to the SHA-3 competition in 2008. It was one of five finalists but wasn't selected (the winner was Keccak). BLAKE reuses the permutation of the ChaCha stream cipher with rotations done in the opposite directions. Some have suspected an advanced optimization, but in fact it originates from a typo in the original BLAKE specifications.

BLAKE2

An evolution of BLAKE proposed shortly after the end of the SHA-3 competition in 2012. It was adopted in many software applications because it's faster than SHA-2 and SHA-3. Several cryptocurrencies' proof-of-work systems use BLAKE2.

BLAKE3

A hash function that combines a reduced-round BLAKE2 and a Merkle tree construction, making it significantly faster than BLAKE2. BLAKE3 was announced at the Real World Crypto 2020 conference.

Bleichenbacher attack

The epitome of a padding oracle attack. Discovered in 1998 by Daniel Bleichenbacher, this is an adaptive chosen-ciphertext attack against the PKCS#1 v1.5 RSA encryption method. Ironically, Bleichenbacher's attack exploits safeguards against other attacks (the mandatory padding bytes) to craft another attack, which after a few million chosen-ciphertext queries allows an attacker to recover a ciphertext's plaintext.

WHY BLEICHENBACHER IS UNPATCHABLE

Typically, when a software security bug and exploit is found and disclosed, a CVE might be issued, the bug is patched, a new version of the software application is released, and users sooner or later update to the new, corrected version. Of course, not all users will or can update immediately after the new release, but most of the time they eventually do.

Bleichenbacher's attack is different because software can't be patched to prevent it. The only effective mitigation is usually to use a different type of RSA encryption, namely PKCS#1 v2.1, aka OAEP, the evolution of the PKCS#1 standards series.

This is why, although Bleichenbacher published his attack in 1998, it was still exploited 20 years later on vulnerable devices as well as in the DROWN attack on legacy TLS versions.

Blind signature

A signature scheme where the signer (knowing the private key) creates a signature without knowing the number signed in a way that randomizes the value that the private key operation is applied to. This is clearer in the straightforward RSA blind signature construction: instead of using md mod N, the signer computes $s_0 = m_0^{\,d}$ where $m_0 = (m \cdot r^e)$ mod N where r is some random value. You can then get the real signature of m by dividing s_0 by r. Details are left as an exercise for you to complete.

This construction might look familiar because it's the same trick the blinding defense uses against side-channel attacks to prevent attackers from controlling the data the private-key operation processes.

Block cipher

A cipher that transforms a block of data to another block of the same length with a key as a parameter. It must be possible to decrypt the block. So the block cipher operation must be bijective (that is, one-to-one and reversible). That's why block ciphers are also *keyed permutations* or *pseudorandom permutations*.

To encrypt more than a single block, which is usually a 64-bit or 128-bit chunk, you need to use a mode of operation (using the ECB mode is usually a bad idea, CBC is better, and CTR or SIV might be even better).

Blockchain

Both a curse and a blessing to cryptography. Comparable to when a subculture goes mainstream and its pioneers miss the old days, and sadly and bitterly contemplate the newly acquired wealth of those who might not deserve it the most.

THANKS, BLOCKCHAIN?

If blockchain revolutionized anything, it's probably the practice, funding, and deployment of cryptography. Thanks to blockchains, we acquired:

- A wealth of new, interesting, nontrivial problems to solve—problems more exciting than designing an nth block cipher. For example, these problems relate to consensus protocols scalability, proof-of-stake security, transactions anonymity (via zk-SNARKS or bulletproofs), cross-blockchain operations, and so on.

- Innovative solutions being created not to be published at peer-reviewed conference and be later forgotten, but actually technologies being deployed at scale, challenged by real threats and engineering constraints rather than only abstract models.

- Large funding available with minimal bureaucracy and formalism, bypassing the traditional grant application systems and its flaws (slowness, misplaced incentives, and work overhead for researchers).

- Passionate people, some without much formal education let alone a PhD, learning advanced cryptography concepts and creating new solutions to new problems, and implementing them without caring about academic rewards.

Blockcipher

An alternative spelling of block cipher, introduced in research papers by Phillip Rogaway.

Blowfish

One of the most popular block ciphers in the 1990s. It owes its recognition to its memorable name and to its designer Bruce Schneier.

BLOWFISH IN HOLLYWOOD

The Blowfish cipher once made it into episodes of the television series *24*. Here's an excerpt from the show's script:

> Mr. O'Brian, a short time ago one of our agents was in touch with Jack Bauer. She sent a name and address that we assume is his next destination. Unfortunately, it's encrypted with Blowfish 148 and no one here knows how to crack that. Therefore, we need your help, please. (. . .)
>
> Show me the file.
>
> Where's your information? 16- or 32-bit word length? 32.
>
> Native or modified data points? Native.
>
> The designer of this algorithm built a backdoor into his code. Decryption's a piece of cake if you know the override codes.

Of course this dialogue makes little sense, and there's no backdoor in Blowfish. Blowfish is actually a secure block cipher, despite the limitation of its 64-bit blocks, and is the core algorithm in the bcrypt password hashing scheme.

BLS (Boneh-Lynn-Shacham) signature

A signature scheme that leverages elliptic-curve pairings, allowing signatures to be shorter than ECDSA and Schnorr signatures. The reason is that each signature consists of a single group element. That is, for a similar security level as a 512-bit ECDSA signature, a BLS signature would be only 256 bits long.

BLS signatures have the useful property of supporting aggregation, whereby multiple public keys and signatures can be combined into a single public key and a single signature, and batch verification can be done efficiently.

Combined with distributed key generation, you can use BLS signatures to build threshold signature schemes, which proved useful in cryptocurrency applications to distribute transaction signatures.

Bob

Subversive stockbroker and Alice's co-conspirator.

🔒 See *Alice*.

Boolean function

A function whose arguments are binary values (that is, either 0 or 1), and that returns a single 0 or 1 bit. For example, $f(a, b, c) = a + b + ac + bc + 1$, where a, b, and c are binary values, is a Boolean function. Here, the plus sign behaves like XOR (because there are only 0s and 1s in Boolean functions), and ab means a times b, which is equivalent to a logical AND operation (giving 1 if and only if $a = b = 1$).

WHY CRYPTOGRAPHERS CARE ABOUT BOOLEAN FUNCTIONS

Boolean functions look dumb until you notice that you could describe any operation—for instance, a hash function—in terms of only Boolean functions. For example, each bit in the output of a hash function is a Boolean function of the input bits. Such functions only exist in the mathematical ether; they're not explicit most of the time. It's practically impossible to compute their polynomial form, let alone to implement and calculate them.

Nonetheless, there are countless research papers about Boolean functions and their security properties: the reason is that when you break a cryptographic hash or block cipher into pieces (meaning rounds and their subcomponents), you'll encounter Boolean functions of a more manageable size—for example, the Boolean functions associated with S-boxes mapping 4-bit blocks to 4-bit blocks. Understanding Boolean functions and their properties, such as nonlinearity and algebraic immunity, has proved critical for designing secure ciphers and breaking weak ones.

Boomerang attack

A differential cryptanalysis technique in which you first *throw* a pair of plaintexts with a given difference into the cipher. You then obtain two ciphertexts and set another difference in these two ciphertexts to obtain two new ciphertexts. Finally, you *catch* the plaintexts obtained by decrypting them. The boomerang attack is essentially a trick to exploit differential characteristics that only cover part of the cipher.

BQP (bounded-error quantum polynomial time)

The class of problems that quantum algorithms, and therefore a hypothetical quantum computer, can efficiently solve. BQP contains problems that classical computers can solve efficiently but also problems that today's computers cannot. The latter are problems for which a superpolynomial quantum speedup exists.

THE HIDDEN SUBGROUP PROBLEM

The most remarkable of the BQP problems, as far as cryptography is concerned, is called the *hidden subgroup problem* (*HSP*). In particular, cryptographers care about its version for commutative (or Abelian) finite groups. We could solve the following problems if HSP for Abelian groups is easy:

🔑 Find p and q given $N = pq$

🔑 Find e given x, p, and x^e mod p

You recognized these problems—factoring and discrete logarithm—whose hardness is necessary to the security of RSA and elliptic-curve cryptography.

Braid group cryptography

An attempt to build a new type of public-key cryptography using non-commutative groups of elements. Such elements can be viewed as braids with a fixed number of strands, and group operations are computationally efficient. As a side benefit, braid group cryptosystems were expected to be resistant to quantum algorithms. But none of the proposed key agreement schemes proved very cryptographically valuable due to their insufficient security.

Brainpool curves

Elliptic curves designed by the German Federal information security authority (*Bundesamt für Sicherheit in der Informationstechnik*, or BSI). Brainpool curves have some suboptimal security properties, but unlike other standards, they provide a 512-bit curve (rather than a 521-bit one).

Break-in recovery

A notion similar to backward secrecy and indistinguishable from future secrecy. The term was coined in the context of the Signal protocol.

🔓 See *Backward secrecy.*

Broadcast encryption

A type of encryption where the same ciphertext is broadcast to a set of receivers so only authorized ones can decrypt it, and receivers can be revoked to no longer decrypt it. Challenges of broadcast encryption are to be secure against collusion of receivers and to minimize ciphertext and keys' lengths.

APPLICATIONS OF BROADCAST ENCRYPTION

Although broadcast encryption was motivated by pay-TV content protection, it was never deployed: the reasons are mainly due to the prohibitive length of ciphertexts or keys and general unsuitability to receivers' security model, where broadcast encryption only addresses a small part of the problems related to piracy.

But broadcast encryption has been used in the AACS content protection scheme used for Blu-ray discs. However, it turned out to be of limited effectiveness against piracy, because the content decryption key (which was protected by broadcast encryption) could be extracted from software players.

Brute-force attack

A type of attack that attempts to recover a secret by consecutively trying all the possible values of that secret. You can start a brute-force attack against most ciphers. But as long as the secret is long enough, the attack will never terminate (unless you're impossibly lucky), because there are too many values to try.

Bulletproof

A zero-knowledge proof proposed as an efficient range proof for cryptocurrencies. The major advantage of bulletproofs is that they don't require a trusted setup. Specifically, they don't need an initialization of the parameters, or *rules of the game*, which must be trusted for the protocol to be secure. Bulletproofs are notably used in Monero.

🔓 See *Range proof*.

Byzantine fault tolerance

An umbrella term for a class of consensus protocols that don't directly rely on mining and proof-of-something. pBFT (and variants thereof) and Tendermint are such protocols; they work by having a fixed number of hosts working together to reliably maintain a common state while distributing trust across hosts.

CAESAR

The Competition for Authenticated Encryption: Security, Applicability, and Robustness, a non-NIST cryptographic competition that took place from 2014 to 2019. Partially funded by but not supervised by NIST, CAESAR identified new authenticated ciphers for several use cases, including *lightweight applications (resource constrained environments)*, *high-performance applications*, and *defense in depth*.

CAESAR'S DEFENSE IN DEPTH FOR AEAD

Of the three use cases defined in the CAESAR competition, defense in depth is probably the least obvious to readers. It was also the most interesting in terms of cryptographic engineering, because it was defined as addressing the following needs:

🔓 Authenticity despite nonce repetition

🔓 Limited privacy damage from nonce repetition

🔓 Authenticity despite release of unverified plaintexts

🔓 Limited privacy damage from release of unverified plaintexts

🔓 Robustness in more scenarios, such as huge amounts of data

Caesar's cipher

An ancient cipher that encrypts a message by shifting each of its letters by three positions, so ABC becomes EFG, CAESAR becomes FDHVDU, and so on. Needless to say, Caesar's cipher isn't very secure.

CAVP (Cryptographic Algorithm Validation Program)

NIST's process to assess that an algorithm's implementation conforms to the standard specification of that algorithm. Prerequisite of a cryptographic module's validation through CMVP in the context of FIPS 140-2 certification. CAVP is essentially about checking test vectors, whereas CMVP covers the other FIPS 140-2 evaluation criteria.

⌂ See *CMVP (Cryptographic Module Validation Program), FIPS 140-2.*

CBC (cipher block chaining)

A mode of operation for block ciphers that has nothing to do with blockchains. CBC encrypts a series of blocks P_i to ciphertext blocks C_i by computing $C_i = \text{Enc}(K, P_i \oplus C_{i-1})$, for $i = 1, \ldots, n$. The initial value of (IV) is C_0, which should be unpredictable to guarantee semantic security. CBC has the useful property that decryption is parallelizable (whereas encryption isn't). Unfortunately, CBC is vulnerable to padding oracle attacks.

CECPQ (combined elliptic-curve and post-quantum)

A hybrid key agreement scheme including an elliptic-curve and a post-quantum scheme. CECPQ was developed by Google as a way to hedge TLS connections against the risks of quantum computing.

The first version, CECPQ1, combined X25519 with the lattice-based scheme NewHope, and was deployed in 2016 for a few months in the Chrome Canary browser. Announced in 2019, CECPQ2 replaces NewHope with the NTRU-based scheme HRSS, and the variant CECPQ2b uses the isogeny-based scheme SIKE.

Cellular automata

Useless in cryptography. It's a source of many bad papers.

Ceremony

A procedure during which important keys, secrets, or sensitive parameters are generated. A ceremony includes procedural and technical security controls to provide assurance about the keys' secure generation and backup—and thus about the software, hardware, processes, and people involved. It's more than picking an acceptable PRNG, which is actually the easiest part. For example, a ceremony involves participants with well-defined roles (such as auditors and operators), a predefined sequence of operations (known as a script or storybook), and the writing of detailed minutes.

Ceremonies are typically held to generate root keys of certificate authorities or master keys (seeds) of blockchain wallets in financial institutions. They are then called *key ceremonies*. Ceremonies can also be called *trusted setups* when they aim to generate parameters of a zero-knowledge proof system.

Certificate

The source of many troubles, including encoding formats, parsing bugs, unrenewed expired certificates, broken chains, untrusted authorities, self signatures, revocation lists, and so on. But often it's the least-bad solution we have.

Certificate authority (CA)

A trusted third party in public-key infrastructures, or the type of component that cryptographers try to avoid but inevitably must live with.

A CA is the entity you must ultimately trust when verifying the validity of a certificate, because the CA can issue certificates as well as intermediate signing certificates. If the CA is compromised, it might grant certificates to malicious entities to perform phishing or man-in-the-middle attacks.

Even some blockchain platforms that claim to be fully decentralized and distributed ultimately rely on a CA.

Certificate transparency (CT)

A Google initiative that reduces the risk from rogue or compromised CAs by creating a public log of certificates being issued. Certificate transparency makes it easier for the domain owner to know whether certificates have been issued for their domain. CT is a kind of public ledger, but it's not a blockchain and has been criticized by blockchain advocates.

ChaCha20

A variant of the Salsa20 stream cipher that is currently one of the most used stream ciphers in the world. This is because it's supported in recent TLS and SSH versions and is the default cipher in many protocols, such as WireGuard.

CHACHA20: BORN ON A FORUM

ChaCha20 was first proposed on the eSTREAM project's discussion forum in a post that began like this:

> I have an idea for improving Salsa20. Obviously, the result isn't an eSTREAM candidate, but I'm curious what people think.

The short post, which didn't attract much interest, described ChaCha20 as potentially having better diffusion and performance.

ChaCha20 did turn out to be slightly faster than Salsa20, thanks to a better use of vectorized SIMD instructions and to better withstand cryptanalysis than its parent algorithm.

CHES (Conference on Cryptographic Hardware and Embedded Systems)

The most *real-world* conference of all IACR conferences before Real World Crypto existed. It's held every year in a different location. Researchers present peer-reviewed research papers with titles such as "Electromagnetic Information Extortion from Electronic Devices Using Interceptor, Its Countermeasure" and "Make Some Noise. Unleashing the Power of Convolutional Neural Networks for Profiled Side-Channel Analysis."

🔒 See *Asiacrypt, CRYPTO, Eurocrypt, FSE, PKC, Real World Crypto, TCC*.

CIA

The three cardinal principles of information security: confidentiality, integrity, and availability. The cryptographer's version of the principles replaces *availability* with *authenticity*.

Ciphertext stealing

A technique to encrypt with a block cipher in CBC mode such that the ciphertext is of the same bit length as the plaintext. Instead of padding the last plaintext block with fixed values, as in PKCS#7 padding, it appends ciphertext bytes from the previous blocks to obtain a full block. It also strips off said bytes of the previous encrypted block to retain the original message size. This trick only works if the message is longer than one block. Standardized by NIST in three different versions (CS1, CS2, and CS3), ciphertext stealing is rarely used in practice, because most of the time a small overhead is acceptable.

Clipper

A simple solution proposed for a complex problem: the Clipper chip aimed to enable encrypted communications for US citizens and businesses while allowing full interception by authorized parties (namely, government and law enforcement). Proposed in the early 1990s by the NSA, the Clipper chip was part of a key escrow architecture where each chip's secret keys would also be shared with US Federal agencies. This has been called a backdoor, but strictly speaking isn't really one because the door's existence wasn't a secret.

In addition to its questionable security architecture, the Clipper chip suffered from a poor technical execution and included a number of security flaws, which helped its opponents halt the project.

CMVP (Cryptographic Module Validation Program)

NIST's process for validating cryptographic modules submitted to the FIPS 140-2 certification. To be evaluated within CMVP, a cryptographic component must implement at least one NIST-standard algorithm.

🔒 See *CAVP (Cryptographic Algorithm Validation Program)*, *FIPS 140-2*.

Code-based cryptography

Post-quantum schemes relying on hardness of decoding a linear code with insufficient information. Many code-based schemes are variants of the 1978 McEliece construction, whose public key describes a random linear code. The encryption process consists of encoding a message while adding some errors to the codeword. Decryption is possible due to a trapdoor that converts the codeword into another code for which decoding is doable.

The submission *Classic McEliece* to NIST's post-quantum competition in 2017 is almost identical to McEliece's 1978 scheme.

Commitment

Also known as bit commitment, a protocol in which a prover temporarily hides a message that cannot be changed. The prover does this by publishing some value that doesn't reveal the value committed (a feature called the *hiding property*) and must also prevent the prover from revealing a different value than the one committed (called the *binding property*). The term *bit commitment* initially referred to coin-flipping protocols in which you commit only one bit. But it's now used for values of any size. The hash values that security people mysteriously post on Twitter so they can claim prior discovery of some 0-day vulnerability are basic commitments.

Concurrent zero-knowledge

Zero-knowledge proofs secure in concurrent settings, that is, when the attacker can observe and disrupt multiple independent executions of the proof protocol.

Consensus protocol

An old concept from the field of distributed computing that became cool again due to its role in blockchain systems.

Control word

A secret key used to encrypt audio and video content in pay-TV systems. This key is 48 bits long in legacy systems, 64 bits long in less old ones, and 128 bits long in the latest generation. Although 48 bits might seem ridiculously short, when the key is changed every 5 or 10 seconds, it can be long enough.

COPACOBANA (Cost-Optimized PArallel COde Breaker)

An academic proof of concept of an FPGA-based DES cracker. Created in approximately 2007, COPACOBANA is capable of breaking a 56-bit DES key within a week in a cost-effective way.

Cothority (collective authority)

A framework for creating decentralized protocols where an operation involves multiple parties so none has greater authority than the others. You can use cothorities to perform operations, such as threshold signature, consensus, or distributed public randomness generation. Although it sounds very blockchain-y, few blockchains have used cothorities.

Cryptanalysis

The practice of analyzing cryptographic algorithms to break them—that is, violate their security assumptions—or to understand why they cannot be broken.

Cryptids

Animals like bigfoots, unicorns, the Kraken, or the Mongolian death worm. As rare as good cryptography software.

Crypto

Shorthand for cryptography and sometimes for cryptocurrency. Use in the latter sense tends to irritate orthodox cryptographers who rally under the banner "crypto is for cryptography."

CRYPTO

The top academic cryptography conference held every summer since 1981 in Santa Barbara, California. Researchers present peer-reviewed papers with titles such as "iO Without Multilinear Maps: New Paradigms via Low-Degree Weak Pseudorandom Generators and Security Amplification" and "Seedless Fruit Is the Sweetest: Random Number Generation, Revisited."

🔒 See *Asiacrypt, CHES, Eurocrypt, FSE, PKC, Real World Crypto, TCC*.

Crypto AG

The "Swiss" company known for literally being owned by the CIA and German intelligence between 1970 and 1994. It allowed the agencies to read the secret communications of several world governments.

THE GREATEST BACKDOOR OF ALL TIME

Governments from Middle Eastern, African, and South American countries would buy encryption equipment from the neutral, supposedly trustworthy Swiss firm, worried that American vendors would spy on them. Unbeknownst to the governments, backdoors in the equipment allowed US intelligence to read all their communications. The NSA deputy director of operations once described the benefits of the operation as follows, allegedly in the late 1980s:

> The mere idea that we might lose any portion of the technical gain and, more importantly, the intelligence made possible by MINERVA is unthinkable . . .

(MINERVA was the codename for Crypto AG.)

Few technical details about the actual backdoors and their exploitation are publicly known. But we do know that, starting in the mid-1960s, Crypto AG's encryption algorithms began relying on feedback shift registers (FSRs).

Interestingly, the NSA used a backdoor technique that consists of choosing parameters in such a way that the output of the stream cipher created from the FSRs is partially predictable because of the existence of short cycles of patterns. In the context of linear FSRs, you can easily achieve this by picking characteristic polynomials with certain properties.

The story of Crypto AG is fascinating, from its foundation in 1952 by Swedish inventor Boris Hagelin to its early ties with the US government and its more recent personalizable encryption machines in the 2000s.

Crypto period

The lifetime of a key in some key management systems, such as the NSA's EKMS. In pay-TV systems, the crypto period is the time during which the same control word (that is, the secret key) is used to encrypt audio and video content. Typical crypto periods are 5 and 10 seconds. These periods might seem short, but they're not short enough to prevent some control-word sharing attacks, whereby the key from one legitimate subscriber is distributed to a large number of pirate boxes.

Crypto variable

The original name for cryptographic keys in the NSA. It was in use until the director of the NSA decided the agency should use the word *key* instead.

Crypto wars

A bellicose term referring to the open disagreements and debates between the US government (and governments of some other Western countries) on the one hand and activists, including researchers and privacy advocates, on the other. The governments wanted more control and surveillance capabilities, typically via proprietary algorithms, export control regulations, key escrow mechanisms, and so on; the latter parties pleading in favor of the right to develop and use any cryptographic mechanism as a way to support privacy rights.

Cryptobiosis

Nothing to do with cryptography but fascinating nonetheless: a near-death state that certain living organisms can enter in response to adverse conditions. When danger subsides, the organisms can return to their original metabolic state. The tardigrade, sometimes used as an allegory for strong cryptography, can enter into cryptobiosis.

Cryptocurrency

🔒 See *Crypto*.

Crypto-Gram

The monthly cryptography digest by Bruce Schneier published since 1998.

Cryptography

🔒 See *Cryptology*.

Cryptologia

Probably the oldest scholarly journal about cryptography; published since 1977.

Cryptology

🔒 See *Cryptography*.

Cryptonomicon

A 1,000-page novel that references cryptography on about every other page. It was written by Neal Stephenson and was published in 1999. It's not very Lovecraftian, despite what its title might suggest.

Unlike other books in which the crypto is mostly made up and laughably unrealistic, *Cryptonomicon* relies on historical facts and genuine cryptographic techniques. Readers might remember the cipher Solitaire (which Bruce Schneier created for the book) and the van Eck phreaking technique.

🔒 See *Solitaire*.

GETTING META

The *Cryptonomicon* is also a fictional book in the real book:

> *They know enough, in other words, to understand that the Cryptonomicon is terribly important, and they have the wit to take the measures necessary to keep it safe. Some of them actually consult it from time to time, and use its wisdom to break Nipponese messages, or even solve whole cryptosystems.*

(. . .)

the Cryptonomicon states that zeta functions are even today being used in cryptography, as sequence generators.

Cryptorchidism

A condition better kept confidential.

Cryptovirology

Popularized by the 2004 book *Malicious Cryptography: Exposing Cryptovirology*. The book describes cryptovirology as "the dark side of cryptography—that device developed to defeat Trojan horses, viruses, password theft, and other cyber-crime (. . .) the art of turning the very methods designed to protect your data into a means of subverting it."

🔒 See *Kleptography*.

CRYPTREC

The Japanese government's Cryptography Research and Evaluation Committees in charge of establishing official cryptography recommendations.

CRYPTREC'S RECOMMENDED CIPHERS

As of 2020, CRYPTREC's top tier is its *e-Government Recommended Ciphers* list, which includes the usual public-key schemes, AES and its usual modes, and the SHA-2 hash functions. In addition to AES, it recommends the block cipher Camellia, as well as the stream cipher KCipher-2.

The middle tier, or the *Candidate Recommended Ciphers* list, notably includes the five block ciphers CIPHERUNICORN, CLEFIA, Hierocrypt, MISTY1, and SC2000. It also includes the SHA-3 hash functions and XOFs, as well as the ChaCha20-Poly1305 authenticated cipher.

The lower tier, the *Monitored Ciphers List*, is a polite way of referring to algorithms you should avoid and includes the usual suspects: SHA-1 and 3DES (but not MD5), as well as RIPEMD160.

CSIDH (Commutative Supersingular Isogeny Diffie–Hellman)

Pronounced *seaside*, the oldest isogeny-based scheme, revisited for efficiency. Also the only post-quantum scheme to have attracted some interest despite a well-known subexponential quantum attack. The proposed parameters "provide relatively little quantum security," in the words of its cryptanalysts; however, its defenders point to its unique applications in the post-quantum arena, such as static key exchange. It's not the same as SIDH.

🔒 See *Diffie–Hellman, Post-quantum cryptography.*

CTF (capture the flag)

A popular competition in the information security community. In the last 15 years, the crypto challenges presented in CTFs have evolved from Vigenère ciphers and visual puzzles to tasks involving state-of-the-art research. For example, participants in the 2020 edition of PlaidCTF had to break an isogeny-based cryptosystem (SIDH) and solve a multivariate system of equations.

Cube attack

A type of higher-order differential cryptanalysis technique, described in 2008 to attack lightweight stream ciphers. The *cube* refers to the combination of bits over which to compute the higher-order differential, extending the notion of a 3D cube to arbitrary dimensions.

WHEN CUBE ATTACKS WORK

In any cryptographic function, each output bit can be expressed as the result of evaluating a polynomial whose input terms are the input bits. If the function is cryptographically strong—and indistinguishable from a random function—this polynomial has exponentially more terms than the number of input bits and so is practically impossible to determine.

But if the function is cryptographically weak, that polynomial might be much simpler, with few terms, and only terms of low algebraic degree (that is, a sum of values that are either input bits or products of two or three input bits). In this case, attackers could use a variant of differential cryptanalysis to determine these terms. Eventually, the attacker could solve the equations to determine the value of secret key bits.

This is what cube attacks do. They were first applied to stream ciphers, which often rely on operations with low algebraic complexity, and thus might lead to cryptographic transforms of low algebraic degree.

Curve25519

A reliable alternative to standardized elliptic curves, albeit somewhat clumsily named: *25519* doesn't refer to the number 25519, but to $2^{255} - 19$, the number of elements in the finite field that Curve25519 is defined over. As a result, there are three types of cryptographers: the *twenty-five five nineteen* ones, the *two five five nineteen* ones, and the *two five five one nine* ones. Fortunately, the curve's technical design is much better than its name thanks to its parameters optimized for speed and safe implementation, as well as its absence of unexplained constants, unlike in NIST curves.

You can use Curve25519 for Diffie–Hellman key agreement, signature, or encryption (via ECIES).

🔒 See *Ed25519, X25519*.

Curve448

A lesser-known little sibling of Curve25519. It provides 224-bit security instead of 128-bit security due to its use of a finite field with $2^{448} - 2^{224} - 1$ elements. Its signature and Diffie–Hellman primitives, Ed448 and X448, are supported in TLS 1.3.

🔒 See *Curve25519*.

Cypher

Alternative spelling of cipher used in pop culture. Its use is considered heresy in academic literature.

Daemon

A misspelling of the last name of Joan Daemen, who co-designed AES and SHA-3.

Davies-Meyer

The most common technique to create a compression function from a block cipher (or keyed permutation). It's used, for example, in MD5,

SHA-1, and SHA-2. Instead of using the block cipher to encrypt as Enc(K, M), you use it to compress a message block M and a hash value H to obtain the new hash value Enc(M, H) $\oplus$ H, where M acts as the cipher's key. Alone, a compression function is a bit useless, but it's easy to turn it into a proper hash function, using, for example, the Merkle–Damgård construction.

In practice, there's no legitimate reason to build your own hash from a block cipher (as an exercise, figure out why it's a bad idea to do so with AES in Davies–Meyer mode); yet the possible use of block ciphers to construct hash functions motivated cryptanalysts to investigate known-key and chosen-key attacks.

Decentralized private computation

A combination of trusted execution and private blockchain token transfer.

Déchiffrer

French for *to decrypt* when you have the key.

Décrypter

French for *to decrypt* when you don't have the key and thus must use cryptanalysis.

Deniable encryption

Randomized public-key encryption where the encrypting party, if coerced to reveal the plaintext and randomness used, can choose different valid combinations of plaintext and randomness, thus preventing self-incrimination.

Deniable encryption can also loosely refer to systems where different keys can decrypt to different legitimate-looking plaintexts, again to dissimulate the real plaintext.

Although motivated by potential real-world problems, deniable encryption is usually not the solution to such problems.

DES (Data Encryption Standard)

The first modern block cipher, standardized by NIST's predecessor, the National Bureau of Standards. It's broken by linear cryptanalysis more efficiently than brute force if you can find 2^{43} plaintext/ciphertext pairs. If not, it's now broken by design because of its too short keys.

Dictionary

A worthless book now that the internet exists.

Dictionary attack

An attack that guesses passwords based on a list of words. Passwords have low entropy because they're often composed of dictionary words and common proper nouns. An attacker can build a list of candidate passwords, ranked in order of popularity, and try them one after another, or in parallel, to find the password that hashes to the value they obtained from some password hash database.

Differential cryptanalysis

The class of cryptanalysis techniques that study the propagation of differences throughout internal computations to exploit some pattern or statistical bias in the output. Most of the attacks on symmetric cryptographic algorithms (block ciphers, hash functions, and so on) are some type of differential cryptanalysis.

The differences exploited might be taken between two input values or between more than two, as in higher-order cryptanalysis and its variants (integral cryptanalysis, cube attacks, and so on). A related technique, linear cryptanalysis, looks a bit different but is ultimately related to differential cryptanalysis. In addition, linear attacks often imply the possibility of pure differential attacks.

Diffie-Hellman

> *Lots of people working in cryptography have no deep concern with real application issues. They are trying to discover things clever enough to write papers about.*
>
> —Whitfield Diffie

A fairly simple mathematical trick that is behind most key agreement protocols, and that indirectly powers many more cryptosystems.

You'll often find security proofs relying on the hardness of the Diffie–Hellman problem (given g^a and g^b, find g^{ab}) or variants thereof.

The *decisional* Diffie–Hellman problem (DDH) was called a "gold mine" by cryptographer Dan Boneh, and was leveraged to build encryption schemes (such as the Cramer–Shoup construction) as well as complex protocols such as threshold signature schemes.

🔒 See *New Directions in Cryptography.*

Disclosure

More effective when the vulnerability is named with a clever acronym and accompanied by a nifty website, including a Q&A and a logo. Researchers first took this approach to tell the world about Heartbleed; then they used it to describe subsequent attacks on SSL/TLS. This allowed them to better communicate the new vulnerability (and spend less time responding to emails from journalists). Notable examples include:

BREACH Browser Reconnaissance and Exfiltration via Adaptive Compression of Hypertext

CRIME Compression Ratio Info-leak Made Easy

DROWN Decrypting RSA with Obsolete and Weakened eNcryption

POODLE Padding Oracle On Downgraded Legacy Encryption

ROBOT Return Of Bleichenbacher's Oracle Threat

Discrete logarithm problem

The problem of finding d in $y = x^d \bmod p$ for a prime p, or in $dG = P$ in elliptic-curve groups of points. The discrete logarithm problem is now the most important computational problem in cryptography, before factoring, because Diffie–Hellman–like protocols have become more common than RSA and Paillier cryptosystems.

Distinguisher

An algorithm used in attacks against a scheme's indistinguishability. For example, if you find a statistical bias in the output of a pseudo-random generator, that bias would serve as a distinguisher, thereby breaking the PRNG.

🔒 See *Indistinguishability*.

Distributed randomness

Randomness generated by a group of parties that don't necessarily trust each other; therefore, they don't want any party to be capable of influencing the outcome. In this context, a simple protocol such as performing an XOR of each participant's random contribution isn't secure. The reason is that the last contributor can set their value to one that, when

XORed with the combination of all previous values, produces the result they want to be returned. Publishing commitments in advance partially addresses the problem.

Dolev-Yao model

The first formal model for defining cryptographic protocols. Also a symbolic framework for describing and analyzing their security. Cryptographers sometimes refer to the Dolev–Yao model when they mean the *active attacker adversarial model*—that is, the model wherein the attacker can eavesdrop, intercept, and modify data transmitted. But the Dolev–Yao model is more than that: it's a general symbolic framework to describe and analyze protocols' security.

Double ratchet

A subprotocol of the Signal messaging protocol. It determines each message's unique keys in such a way that an attacker who knows the message keys at a given time can determine neither past nor future message keys, thereby providing forward secrecy and some form of backward secrecy.

🔒 See *Signal protocol.*

ONE RATCHET, TWO RATCHETS

The double ratchet is a highly stateful protocol. It's called *double* because it combines two techniques:

- 🔑 The *symmetric-key ratchet*, which maintains a hash chain from which message keys are derived.
- 🔑 The *Diffie-Hellman ratchet*, which performs Diffie–Hellman key exchanges with ephemeral key pairs to make future states unpredictable.

Dragonfly

PAKE defined for the authentication standard EAP-pwd used in the Wi-Fi security suite WPA3. Attackers can bypass implementations of Dragonfly by exploiting the timing side channels in the hash-to-curve operations.

🔒 See *PAKE (password-authenticated key agreement).*

DRBG (deterministic random bit generator)

An oxymoronic-sounding term referring to a component that deterministically generates a long string of random-looking bits when given some actually random value (called a *seed*, a *key*, or sometimes just *entropy*). An operating system's random generator usually includes an entropy extraction mechanism that generates some unpredictable bits from some analog source and pushes these bits to an entropy pool from which a DRBG takes its seed.

A DRBG is different from a PRNG; the terms PRBG and DRNG are rarely used.

🔒 See *Pseudorandom generator (PRNG)*.

DSA (Digital Signature Algorithm)

The public-key signature scheme designed and patented by the NSA. It was standardized as part of the DSS (Digital Signature Standard) in 1991. This choice drew some criticism to which NIST responded as follows in the magazine *Federal Computer Week*:

> NIST made the final choice. We obtained technical assistance from NSA, and we received technical inputs from others as well, but [NIST] made the final choice.

At the time, the criticisms of DSA were about its efficiency, incompleteness (it didn't specify a hash function), risk of patent infringement, and security.

🔒 See *DSS (Digital Signature Standard)*.

DSS (Digital Signature Standard)

The name of the NIST standard about digital signatures; not a single algorithm.

In 1982, NIST (then called the NBS) published a "Solicitation for Public Key Cryptographic Algorithms." NIST later did the same for block ciphers and hash functions, resulting in the AES and SHA-3 standards. In 1987, NIST cancelled the DSS project upon request from the NSA. The standardization effort later resumed, leading to several standards established in 1991, including the NSA-designed DSA.

DSS is also the abbreviation of the sodium trimethylsilylpropanesulfonate chemical compound, which is somehow related to cryptography.

DVB-CSA

The Common Scrambling Algorithm: an algorithm standardized by the Digital Video Broadcasting consortium to protect video content in pay-TV systems, typically by encrypting MPEG transport stream packets.

🔓 See *Control word.*

VERSIONS OF DVB-CSA

The first version of the DVB-CSA standard, called *CSA1*, combines a stream cipher and a block cipher, and has a 48-bit key. CSA2 is similar but has a longer key of 64 bits. If these key sizes sound short to you, keep in mind that for most live content, the key usually changes every 5 or 10 seconds.

CSA3 is very different. Although its full design isn't public, it's known to combine AES with another (patented) block cipher running in some unusual operation mode. Additionally, it includes components designed to prevent software emulation. Per its design, CSA3 should run in dedicated hardware circuits only, like those found in the systems-on-chip of set-top boxes.

E0

A stream cipher used in Bluetooth. Broken in theory but not in practice. The more recent Bluetooth Low Energy standard uses AES-CCM instead.

ECB (electronic codebook)

The most obvious way to use a block cipher, where each block is processed independently of the others. ECB is the most robust mode against repeated IVs and nonces. But everybody knows ECB is insecure because you can see the penguin.

ECC

An acronym for either elliptic-curve cryptography or error-correcting code, depending on the context; confusion between the two can lead to unfortunate situations.

🔓 See *Elliptic-curve cryptography.*

ECDLP (Elliptic-curve discrete logarithm problem)

Arguably the most important computational problem as far as cryptographic security is concerned: given the points P and xP, find the number x, where multiplication happens in the group of an elliptic curve over a finite field.

Elliptic-curve schemes have replaced many instances of RSA or classical Diffie–Hellman, for example, in the TLS 1.3 standard.

ECDSA (Elliptic-curve DSA)

The elliptic-curve counterpart of DSA, whose security requires the hardness of ECDLP, but is not totally equivalent to it. As far as we know, ECDLP's hardness only implies ECDSA's security (unforgeability) in the generic group model, which is an abstraction of ECDSA but not exactly ECDSA.

🔒 See *DSA (Digital Signature Algorithm)*.

ECDSA IN THE PLAYSTATION 3

Many people first learned about the ECDSA algorithm after attackers discovered that the PlayStation 3 used a weak implementation of it. The implementation's nonce—an argument supposed to be unique for each signature, typically by being chosen at random—remained the same, allowing the attackers to easily retrieve the private key.

(Spoiler: the key was 46 DC EA D3 17 FE 45 D8 09 23 EB 97 E4 95 64 10 D4 CD B2 C2.)

Those who missed the PS3 hack later discovered ECDSA as the signature algorithm in Bitcoin and Ethereum, where ECDSA keys were sometimes also compromised because of repeated or biased nonces in flawed wallet software.

ECIES (Elliptic-curve IES)

The elliptic-curve version of the IES public-key encryption scheme. Like IES, ECIES is a hybrid encryption scheme, therefore it needs a symmetric cipher to actually encrypt messages.

🔒 See *IES (Integrated Encryption Scheme)*.

Ed25519

EdDSA signatures using Curve25519's Edwards representation rather than the Montgomery format used by X25519, which causes developers a lot of headaches.

🔓 See *Curve25519, EdDSA.*

EdDSA

A deterministic elliptic-curve signature scheme based on Schnorr's scheme. The main alternative to the ECDSA standard. In its purest form, it's resilient to non-collision-resistant hash functions and is famously used by Ed25519.

EKMS (Electronic Key Management System)

A legacy key management system designed by NSA to secure communications for the US Army and other organizations.

TOO MANY KEYS

If you thought key management for web applications was hard, wait until you have to do it in an environment with different classification levels, networks, device types, data management policies, and staff training.

The following (incomplete) list of EKMS key abbreviations illustrates the complexity of managing keys in its target environments:

🔑 AEK: Algorithmic encryption key

🔑 KEK: Key encryption key

🔑 KPK: Key production key

🔑 OWK: Over the wire key

🔑 TEK: Traffic encryption key

🔑 TrKEK: Transmission key encryption key

🔑 TSK: Transmission security key

The system classifies keys depending on their role (operational, maintenance, or test). Operational keys, in turn, can have a variety of different attributes: they can be emergency contingency keys, joint theater keys, or allied keys, among others.

Electronic codebook

A cipher, in archaic NSA parlance. For example: "Electronic codebooks, such as the Advanced Encryption Standard, are both widely used and difficult to attack cryptanalytically."

ElGamal

For many years, the only public-key encryption scheme used and taught in crypto classes other than RSA. Introduced in the 1985 article "A Public Key Cryptosystem and a Signature Scheme Based on Discrete Logarithms," which modestly started with the following abstract:

> A new signature scheme is proposed together with an implementation of the Diffie–Hellman key distribution scheme that achieves a public key cryptosystem. The security of both systems relies on the difficulty of computing discrete logarithms over finite fields.

ECDSA eventually overshadowed the signature scheme, and currently, ElGamal encryption is rarely used. Instead, cryptographers use ECIES except in applications in which the message must be directly public-key-encrypted (as in some e-voting systems).

The in-the-exponent variant of ElGamal encryption has two interesting properties: it is additively homomorphic, and decryption is impossible (unless you solve a discrete logarithm problem). Despite the latter suboptimal property, this version proved useful in threshold signature schemes.

Elligator

A method of encoding elliptic-curve points as random-looking strings to make public keys indistinguishable from encrypted data.

Elliptic curve

Not an ellipsis, not a curved line. A set of points on the plane whose (x, y) coordinates satisfy the curve's equation, which usually has the form $y^2 = x^3 + ax + b$, where a and b are fixed parameters. Cryptographic applications only work with points whose coordinates belong to some finite field; therefore, the curve has a finite set of points.

Elliptic curves were, of course, discovered before cryptography, and mathematicians studied them much earlier. For example, elliptic curves played a role in the proof of Fermat's Last Theorem.

Cryptography takes advantage of the fact that an elliptic curve's points happen to form a group structure with respect to a geometrically defined group operation, denoted as point addition. For well-chosen curve types, the equivalent of the discrete logarithm problem becomes difficult in such groups, which is why these curves prove useful in public-key cryptography.

Elliptic-curve cryptography

Public-key cryptography relying on elliptic curves and related hardness problems (the discrete logarithm, or a variant thereof). Elliptic-curve cryptography can do almost everything that legacy public-key cryptography can do, in a way that is often faster and uses shorter keys. That includes encryption, key agreement, and signature. In addition, you can use it for more exotic cryptographic schemes due to its support of pairings.

🔓 See *Pairing-based cryptography.*

Encipherment

A synonym of encryption with emphasis on the act and operations carried out during the encryption process. *To encipher,* like the French verb *chiffrer,* comes from the Arabic صفر (*sifr,* the digit zero), whereas *to encrypt,* like the verb *crypter,* comes from the Greek *kryptos* (concealed, secret).

End-to-end encryption (E2EE)

Encryption is said to be end-to-end when only the dedicated recipient(s) can decrypt the messages. It sounds straightforward but is actually an arduous engineering problem.

As usual in cryptography, the hard part of such a system is key management and distribution, not the actual encryption, which is why many E2EE systems need a central server. Many E2EE systems also rely on trust-but-verify mechanisms and are only end-to-end as long as participants perform some manual verification, such as checking a conversation's fingerprint.

In addition, E2EE systems sometimes ultimately rely on a central CA to enable trusted TLS connections (which you can think of as simply end-to-end encryption over the transport layer rather than the application layer).

Enigma

The electromechanical encryption machine used by the Nazis during World War II. The Enigma was analyzed by Polish and British cryptanalysts, including Alan Turing, using techniques that researchers would later rediscover and call differential cryptanalysis, related-key attacks, and side-channel attacks.

Entropy

A notion introduced around 1865 by Rudolf Clausius, arguably the founder of modern thermodynamics. But entropy wasn't named until three years after his first formalization of the second law of thermodynamics (which states that entropy, at a microscopic level, cannot decrease in a closed system). Claude Shannon's concept of information entropy came much later in his famous 1948 paper. Cryptography uses information entropy to assess a cryptosystem's security by quantifying its amount of uncertainty.

INFORMATION ENTROPY

Entropy is a property of a probability distribution, not of any particular value in that distribution. That is why asking about the entropy of some random-looking value makes no sense unless you know how this value was chosen and from which distribution.

In the context of information theory, Shannon's entropy of some random variable X is defined as

$$H(X) = -\sum_{n} P_n \log_2 P_n$$

over a finite set of observables n, where P_n is the probability of the event n.

In the case of a continuous random variable, we can extend the entropy definition to

$$-\int_S P(x) \log_2 P(x)dx$$

where $P(x)$ is the variable's density function, and S is the support set of the random variable.

When a symmetric cipher has an n-bit key, where all n-bit values are valid and equiprobable through key generation, a random key's entropy is n. In public-key schemes, the entropy of a private key will rarely be equal to its encoding's bit length, because not all values of that length might be valid keys.

ePrint

Officially the Cryptology ePrint Archive, at *https://eprint.iacr.org/*. A website where cryptography researchers can post their papers online prior to formal, double-blind, peer-reviewed publication and be sure they'll be noticed. Most cryptography researchers check the new papers published on ePrint at least once a week.

Erathosthenes' sieve

A method of enumerating all prime numbers up to some upper bound; a 2,000-year-old algorithm typically taught in high school. It was rediscovered during the Black Hat 2019 conference.

eSTREAM

A cryptography competition, officially a *project*, organized by the EU-funded ECRYPT project between 2004 and 2008. Of the 34 submitted ciphers, eight made it to the final portfolio, which included two categories: software (those with 128-bit keys) and hardware (those with 80-bit keys). By far the most successful design from eSTREAM is Salsa20, a cipher that later evolved to ChaCha20, which became central to the BLAKE family of hash functions. Of the other portfolio ciphers, Trivium and Grain (or variants thereof) are used in niche applications, and F-FCSR was broken.

🔒 See *Grain, Salsa20, Trivium*.

Ethereum

An important blockchain platform for decentralized applications, such as tokens. Ethereum has led to some of the most interesting cryptography research and open problems, based on novel challenges faced by their unique decentralized deployment, adversarial model, and Turing-complete functionality. For example, consider the following, all of which are admittedly more exciting than yet another new block cipher: proof-of-stake security, smart contract formal verification, atomic swaps, and sharding.

Eurocrypt

Europe's largest academic cryptography conference, held every spring in a different European location since 1987. Researchers present peer-reviewed research papers with titles such as "Indistinguishability Obfuscation Without Multilinear Maps: New Methods for Bootstrapping and Instantiation" and "A Quantum-Proof Non-Malleable Extractor with Application to Privacy Amplification Against Active Quantum Adversaries."

🔒 See *Asiacrypt, CHES, CRYPTO, FSE, PKC, Real World Crypto, TCC.*

Eve

Alice and Bob's nemesis.

🔒 See *Alice, Bob.*

E-voting

A topic that cryptographers like to publish papers about but don't like to see deployed in reality because it's perceived as unacceptably risky. E-voting is nonetheless cryptographically fascinating. It involves non-trivial cryptography, such as homomorphic encryption schemes used to encrypt ballots and aggregate them in a privacy-preserving way, and noninteractive zero-knowledge proofs, which are used to prove a vote's correctness.

Factoring problem

Given $n = pq$, find the primes p and q. Easy to solve if you have a large enough quantum computer.

Feedback shift register

An array of values, usually bits or bytes, that updates by shifting the values over and then filling the empty slot with the result of some function of the previous state's values. Historically, this cipher mechanism came after electromechanical machines and preceded modern ciphers. It's still used in some hardware-oriented algorithms and in the mobile communication standard SNOW 3G.

There are two kinds of feedback shift registers. In linear ones (LFSRs), this update function is linear, which renders the output predictable but can also provide guarantees that the period of LFSR is maximal. In nonlinear ones (NFSRs), after a few cycles of updates, the output values are highly nonlinear functions of the initial state, but guarantees on the period are difficult to compute. Concretely, linear update functions only do additions, whereas nonlinear ones do additions and multiplications.

A good design strategy is to combine LFSRs and NFSRs.

🔒 See *Grain, SNOW 3G, Trivium.*

Feistel network

A method of constructing a block cipher from a smaller block cipher or hash function. It works by splitting the message block in two halves, L and R, and updating it by repeatedly replacing (L, R) with $(R, L \oplus f(R))$, where $f()$ is the smaller function and can take a secret value as a parameter. Feistel network is sometimes called *Luby–Rackoff construction* after the researchers who formally analyzed its security. The XOR operation can be replaced by another group operation.

🔒 See *DES (Data Encryption Standard), Lucifer.*

Fialka (Фиалка)

The Soviet counterpart to the Enigma machine created after World War II. Unlike Western encryption machines, Фиалка supported Cyrillic characters.

Fiat-Shamir

A technique for turning an interactive proof (a protocol between a prover and a verifier that involves multiple rounds) into a noninteractive one (a single message from the prover) using hash functions.

FIPS 140-2

A set of security requirements for cryptographic modules (software or hardware), established by NIST in 2001. It's been superseded by FIPS 140-3 since 2019.

WHAT FIPS 140-2 REALLY MEANS

When a vendor says "We are FIPS 140-2 certified," the statement can have one of two meanings: "We have applied for the certification," or, ideally, "We have received the certification."

The latter case can also have different meanings:

☞ Level 1: Correctness of the FIPS-approved algorithms.

☞ Level 2: Level 1 plus some tamper evidence—for example, the ability to detect physical attacks after they occur by observing broken seals on the box.

☞ Level 3: Level 2 plus some tamper detection—for example, the platform's ability to detect physical attacks in real time and reset itself to factory mode if it believes it's under attack. This level also includes some physical isolation and stronger authentication.

☞ Level 4: Level 3 plus some stronger tamper detection with the guarantee that the module will detect most physical attack attempts and reset itself when under attack (for instance, by zeroizing secrets).

It's worth noting that FIPS 140-2 doesn't measure a system's resilience to physical attacks so much as the system's ability to detect them. This acknowledges that most systems are vulnerable to physical attacks given the right equipment.

Additionally, the fact that a system is FIPS 140-2 certified doesn't mean that it's perfectly secure. The reason is that 1) FIPS 140-2 is limited by its scope and by the definition of the security requirements of each of its levels, and 2) even in a certified product, the certification usually only applies the cryptographic module (and sometimes only parts of it). In other words, if some application calls a FIPS 140-2 Level 3 module to encrypt some message, and the application's software has a flaw that leaks said plaintext, don't blame the certification.

FIPS 140-3

New version of FIPS 140-2 since 2019. It introduces requirements against noninvasive attacks and the concepts of *Normal Operation* and *Degraded Operation*, among others.

🔒 See *FIPS 140-2*.

Forgery

An attack whose goal is not to recover some secret but to create a supposedly hard-to-generate value without the knowledge of some secret. Unforgeability is the corresponding security notion and is most commonly associated with signatures and MACs. More generally, unforgeability must apply to any scheme for which an attacker should have trouble creating a valid output. These include ciphertexts in authentication encryption and zero-knowledge proof protocol transcripts.

Sometimes forgeability is a desirable property (for example, to achieve deniability.

Formal verification

A form of testing that relies on mathematical guarantees. Applied to security protocols, formal verification includes symbolic and computational verification techniques, which assess whether a protocol satisfies properties such as confidentiality and authentication. Another example is programming languages that can certify that an implementation is functionally correct with respect to a specification, or that it's free of certain classes of side channels.

High-assurance applications often receive some sort of formal verification, such as the Common Criteria security evaluation framework's EAL7 assurance level. Still, don't be fooled into thinking formal verification means *proof that everything about a crypto implementation is secure.*

Format-preserving encryption

A type of encryption that produces a ciphertext with the same format as the original message. For example, the format-preserving encryption of a 16-digit credit card number would produce another 16-digit number. Format-preserving encryption is often useful for encrypting database entries whose field type must have a specific format, such as social security numbers, IP addresses, and ZIP codes. Although the problem sounds simple, it requires sophisticated techniques, especially for the more general problem of creating ciphers from arbitrary domains of values.

Forward secrecy

The notion that something remains secure if something else is compromised at a later time. What counts as *something*, *something else*, and *a later time* depends on the context. Forward secrecy is usually a relevant security notion for key agreement protocols, secure messaging protocols (and their ratchetting mechanisms), pseudorandom generators, pseudorandom functions, MACs, and other stateful objects.

It's usually easier to achieve forward secrecy than backward secrecy, because it's easier to erase the past than to make the future unpredictable (in cryptography, at least).

🔓 See *Backward secrecy.*

FOX

🔓 See *IDEA NXT.*

FSE (Fast Software Encryption)

A conference focused on the design and cryptanalysis of symmetric cryptography primitives, including slow and hardware-oriented hash functions. FSE is sometimes viewed as an applied cryptography conference, despite the fact that it rarely focuses on real-world algorithms, let alone real-world attacks.

Researchers present peer-reviewed papers with titles such as "Improving the MILP-Based Security Evaluation Algorithm Against Differential/Linear Cryptanalysis Using a Divide-and-Conquer Approach" and "Low AND Depth and Efficient Inverses: A Guide on S-boxes for Low-Latency Masking."

🔓 See *Asiacrypt, CHES, CRYPTO, Eurocrypt, PKC, Real World Crypto, TCC.*

Fully homomorphic encryption

🔓 See *Homomorphic encryption.*

Functional encryption

A type of cryptographic scheme that looks like magic: when designed for some function $f()$, decrypting $Enc(M)$ yields not M but $f(M)$. But like many of the magic cryptographic schemes, it's of limited use in practice, because it can efficiently support only simple functionalities.

To build functional encryption schemes, cryptographers can use the trick of leveraging indistinguishability obfuscation: in other words, the decryption process that finds $f(M)$ would consist of an obfuscated program that first retrieves M and then computes $f(M)$ without ever exposing M.

Future secrecy

A term coined in the context of the Signal protocol to refer to a notion similar to backward secrecy. Indistinguishable from break-in recovery.

🔒 See *Backward secrecy.*

Fuzzy extractor

A scheme for extracting the value of some high-entropy secret from multiple noisy readings, each with different random errors, to derive a key. This might sound a lot like an error-correcting code, but it's different: first, the value read is not a codeword (which has redundancy in it and thus is suboptimal entropy), but instead is a value of potentially maximal entropy; second, the value is not read once but multiple times; and third, the enrollment data used to decode the secret must not leak information about said secret. Therefore, you can store it without privacy leaks.

You might find fuzzy extractors used in biometric authentication applications, which have to extract a value that uniquely identifies an individual. These applications typically must extract this value from noisy measurements and without relying on a database of sensitive data, such as data about each individual. Conversely, in a traditional approach to authentication, you would compare a new measurement to a registered one to identify a person.

Generalized birthday problem

The problem of finding values $X_1, \ldots, X_k$ such that $\text{Hash}(X_1) \oplus \cdots \oplus \text{Hash}(X_k) = 0$. The special case of a classical collision is that of finding two distinct values, such that $\text{Hash}(X_1) \oplus \text{Hash}(X_2) = 0$. The *birthday attack* finds such pairs in $O(2^{n/2})$ queries to the hash function, where n is the output bit size.

In the generalized birthday problem, it's easy to see that the larger the value k, the easier the problem. More precisely, the cost of a collision becomes $O(k2^{n/(1+\log_2 k)})$ time and space, or of the order of $2^{n/3}$ for $k = 4$.

GNFS (General Number Field Sieve)

The best (nonquantum) algorithm for factoring large integers.

GOST

The USSR national standard block cipher designed in the 1970s and included in the GOST 28147-89 standard series. Whereas the American DES cipher, designed in the same era, uses keys that are only 64 bits long, GOST works with 256-bit keys and comes with customizable S-boxes. Constructed as a Feistel network like DES, GOST hasn't been meaningfully broken, although research papers have described some attacks against it that perform fewer than 2^{256} operations. Russian authorities officially deprecated GOST in 2019. Its successor is the block cipher Кузнечик (Kuznyechik).

Grain

A family of minimalistic hardware-oriented stream ciphers: Grain (80-bit key), Grain 128, and Grain 128a (128-bit key).

Gröbner basis

A canonical representation of a system of multivariate equations. Computing a Gröbner basis for a multivariate system is one of the possible definitions of "solving" it, because it can be used, for example, to find its numeric solutions.

The general problem of computing Gröbner bases is NP-hard. The actual time and memory required to compute one for a specific system of equations, as found in multivariate cryptography or in algebraic cryptanalysis, is usually large and hard to estimate: but when it's not, it produces spectacular cryptanalyses.

Group signature

A signature scheme involving a group of potential signers. Any group member can issue a signature on behalf of the group, and a verifier can learn the identity of the group members but not of the actual signer. There's an exception: groups must work with a trusted entity, called the *group manager*, which can trace signatures back to their original signer. Ring signatures don't have this traceability property or the need for a group manager.

🔒 See *Ring signature*.

Grover's algorithm

A quantum algorithm that in theory can break symmetric ciphers in $O(2^{n/2})$ instead of $O(2^n)$ complexity, where n is the key length.

Hardcore predicate

A key concept in the theoretical definition of one-way functions and permutations: for some one-way function $f()$, a hardcore predicate is some bit of information about an input x that is easy to compute from x but hard from $f(x)$. By definition, you should be able to find a hardcore predicate for any given one-way function and its permutations.

Hash function

The simplest cryptographic object, and at first glance, the dumbest operation ever. A hash function takes a single input of any type, format, or size, and returns a single output that is a fixed size and looks totally unrelated to its input. Yet equipped with such a trivial tool, you can construct secure symmetric ciphers, pseudorandom generators, key derivation functions, and even public-key signatures, as well as a variety of security protocols.

Hash-based cryptography

The most secure but slowest form of post-quantum cryptography. You can use hash functions to create various cryptographic objects, such as stream ciphers or pseudorandom generators. But when you hear *hash-based cryptography*, it refers to public-key signatures built from only hash functions.

Simple hash-based signatures, as proposed by Lamport, Merkle, and Winternitz in the late 1970s, have severe shortcomings. For example, you can use them only a limited number of times or only on very short messages. Like many problems in computer science, researchers have addressed the problem of scaling hash-based signatures by throwing trees, trees, and even more trees at it. This has notably led to the SPHINCS and XMSS designs.

🔒 See *SPHINCS, XMSS.*

Heartbleed

The bug in OpenSSL that revived interest in the security of TLS and its implementation. Ultimately, Heartbleed led to a safer OpenSSL, as well as the TLS 1.3 protocol.

Hedged signature

A type of signature that reintroduces randomness as a defense against fault attacks. Fault attacks affect signature schemes, such as EdDSA and deterministic ECDSA, that don't need a random or unique value to be secure. (By contrast, ECDSA requires a fresh secret random value per signature.) Such derandomized signature schemes protect against poor randomness but have been shown to be vulnerable to fault attacks that partially exploit their determinism. Hedged signatures aim to correct this without allowing lower-quality randomness to reduce the scheme's security. Such hedged signatures include the XEdDSA variant, as well as the post-quantum schemes qTESLA and Picnic2.

HFE (Hidden Field Equations)

A family of multivariate public-key schemes, including encryption and signature schemes. As modestly stated in the 1996 paper that introduced it, "the security of HFE is not proved but *apparently* it seems to be related to the problem of solving a system of multivariate quadratic equations over a finite field."

HMAC (Hash-based MAC)

For many developers, a synonym of *MAC*. Strictly speaking, however, an HMAC isn't a MAC but a way to construct a MAC from a hash function.

For example, you can construct a MAC atop SHA-256, which is called *HMAC-SHA-256*. Keep in mind that HMACs are not the only— and not necessarily the best—ways of constructing MACs.

Homomorphic encryption

An encryption that satisfies $\text{Dec}(\text{Enc}(M_1) \otimes \text{Enc}(M_2)) = M_1 \odot M_2$ for some operators $\otimes$ and $\odot$ that might be identical or distinct, and are usually some type of addition or multiplication. For example, encrypting a message with textbook RSA by doing $M^d \bmod n$ for some message M is homomorphic with respect to multiplication: the product of two ciphertexts is the ciphertext of the product of the plaintexts.

Homomorphism can be a security issue and a feature, depending on the context. For example, certain e-voting systems leverage the homomorphic property of Paillier's cryptosystem to aggregate ballots without decrypting them individually.

Fully homomorphic encryption is a more general and powerful property but is also harder to realize: a fully homomorphic encryption can be homomorphic with respect to any operation performed on the ciphertext instead of just a single group operation.

HPC (Hasty Pudding Cipher)

A mostly forgotten block cipher submitted in 1998 to the AES competition. Its designer called it "the first Omni-Cipher: It can encrypt any blocksize with any keysize."

Unconventional yet innovative, HPC had several unique features as it was:

- The first tweakable block cipher (the tweak was then called the *spice* or the *secondary key*)
- Optimized for 64-bit architectures and the fastest of all AES candidates on these
- Able to support any key and block size
- Composed of five subciphers: HPC-Tiny, -Short, -Medium, -Long, and -Extended

The so-called *spice* anticipated some of the future needs for a tweak. As the specification comments:

> HPC's spice is an important protection for short-block encryption: The spice can be different for every bit field, preventing dictionary attacks.

In addition, HPC's designer foresaw that one of the main applications of encryption would be online videos:

> The most important future application for encryption will be for video communications, on stock hardware, which will be 64-bit machines. The Hasty Pudding Cipher is the fastest cipher for bulk encryption on 64-bit machines. (. . .) Performance in video applications is so important that HPC should be the primary AES choice.

Although it remains unbroken—only equivalent keys were found—HPC wasn't selected as the AES and didn't even make it to the second round. Its unorthodox design and lack of formal security arguments probably didn't play in its favor.

HSM (hardware security module)

Hardware equipment dedicated to running cryptographic operations and other security tasks. HSMs can come in different form factors, such as rack servers or USB dongles. HSMs don't necessarily run cryptographic operations using dedicated hardware (as in a dedicated silicon circuit). Actually, most of the time, they run all cryptography in software, executed by some general-purpose processor. The S in HSM refers to the functionality it implements; it doesn't necessarily mean the HSM is more secure than a normal computer.

HTTP/3

🔒 See QUIC *(Quick UDP Internet Connections)*.

Hyperelliptic-curve cryptography

Like elliptic-curve cryptography but using a higher-dimensional object: the Jacobian of a hyperelliptic curve. We can't explain what a Jacobian is in terms of anything else that is familiar to most readers, to paraphrase Richard Feynman.

The main advantage of hyperelliptic curves is that, owing to the additional dimensions, the same finite field generates larger groups than it would with an elliptic curve. This strength is also a weakness: when the number of dimensions becomes too high (usually more than three), discrete logarithms become easier.

IACR (International Association for Cryptologic Research)

Cryptographers' union, a nonprofit that organizes the largest academic cryptography conferences and manages the reference preprint platform ePrint.

IDEA (International Data Encryption Algorithm)

A 64-bit block cipher from the early 1990s. One of the rare block ciphers that uses the Lai–Massey construction, not a Feistel or substitution–permutation network.

Despite a rather heuristic design approach, IDEA resisted cryptanalysis for years. The first attack against it that proved potentially faster than brute force didn't appear until 2012. (This was a biclique attack with 2^{126} operations.)

IDEA is one of the few ciphers that uses integer multiplication operations, which has some security benefits but makes protecting against side-channel attacks difficult.

IDEA NXT

A block cipher with little similarity to IDEA except for their shared Lai–Massey construction. Also like IDEA, it was designed for the Mediacrypt AG company and patented. Initially named and published as FOX, IDEA NXT proved very useful in antipiracy initiatives, not only because of its cryptographic merits.

Identity-based encryption

A means of sending an encrypted message without knowing someone's public key. For instance, when Alice wants to send an encrypted message to Bob but doesn't know his public key, identity-based encryption (IBE) allows her to compute it using the name *Bob* and some master public key. The only caveat is that IBE requires a trusted third party, called the *key server*, which knows some master private key and uses it to generate users' private keys. Bob therefore needs to authenticate to the key server, proving that he's the real Bob, to receive his private key.

IES (Integrated Encryption Scheme)

A public-key encryption scheme that doesn't involve a public-key encryption primitive. Instead, the sender chooses a random key pair, computes a Diffie–Hellman shared secret between the fresh private key and the recipient's public key, derives a symmetric key from it, and encrypts the message with some authenticated cipher. Neither party performs a public-key operation to encrypt the data.

Impatient saboteur

In the Dolev–Yao model, an archetypal attacker who can transmit data but not receive it. Or in Dolev and Yao's own words, "one who only initiates conversations (and does not rely on being spoken to.)"

Impossibility

Cryptographer Moti Yung once said, "When a software engineer says [a security engineering problem] is impossible, that really just means it's cryptographically interesting."

Impossible differential attack

A differential attack that exploits abnormally unlikely events rather than abnormally likely ones. Differential cryptanalysis generally exploits patterns of unusually high probability that occur in the differences between outputs and inputs with a specific difference. Impossible differential attacks exploit the opposite type of pattern, namely those that have zero chance of being observed under certain conditions. If cryptanalysts notice these patterns, they can deduce that the condition doesn't hold. This information could help recover a cipher's secret key or subkey.

IND-CCA

Indistinguishability of ciphertexts under chosen-ciphertext attacks. The strongest security notion for encryption schemes (both public-key and symmetric-key schemes). The chosen-ciphertext might intuitively make little sense in practice. The reason is that you'll rarely find systems where attackers can decrypt any ciphertexts they want, but encryption that can do more can do less. In addition, there are cases in which you do have a decryption oracle, such as some DRM systems.

IND-CPA

Indistinguishability of ciphertexts under chosen-plaintext attacks. Also known as semantic security. It's the idea that a ciphertext shouldn't reveal anything about a plaintext other than its approximate length, even to an active attacker capable of retrieving the ciphertext corresponding to the plaintexts of their choice.

IND-CPA is the standard security notion for symmetric encryption. For example, block ciphers in CTR or in CBC mode are secure if the underlying block cipher is secure, and if CTR nonces are unique or CBC initial values are unpredictable. That's a lot of ifs, which in practice can lead to security flaws in otherwise IND-CPA schemes.

Indelibility

Property belonging to a transaction, or series thereof, that is time-stamped implicitly or explicitly and cannot be backdated or otherwise altered. Cryptographic ledger mechanisms, such as blockchains, can often address this problem.

Indifferentiability

Property of a construction, such as of a hash function, that is guaranteed to lead to a secure primitive if the building blocks have no security flaw. In the context of hash functions, we talk of *indifferentiability from a random oracle*, meaning that if the underlying compression function or permutation is ideal, the hash function has as many structural properties as a random oracle: that is, none.

Indistinguishability

The property in which something that isn't really random appears the same as something that is actually random. If the two are indistinguishable, you cannot extract information from the not-really-random thing. In the case of encryption, the not-really-random thing is the ciphertext, and the information you're unable to extract is about the plaintext. Indistinguishability applies to other cryptographic functionalities as well.

Indistinguishability obfuscation (iO)

The mathematization of the intuitive concept of software obfuscation. In cryptography, as in software security, the obfuscation process takes as input a program and produces a second program that in some sense hides how the first program works: its internal variables, secret arguments, and so on. Unlike in software security, cryptography sees a program as one of the possible abstract representations, most commonly a Boolean circuit with AND, OR, and NOT gates.

iO can be seen as a raw encoding of the input–output relations that hides its implementation details, such as subprocedures or intermediate variables. The notion of indistinguishability is just a formal way to express the idea that, given obfuscations of two distinct yet equivalent programs, an attacker shouldn't be able to identify which of the programs is which.

Although iO sounds like the solution to many problems, in practice it's not because of its high complexity and inefficiency.

Information-theoretic security

Security that even infinite computational power cannot compromise. For example, imagine that you encrypt some 128-bit secret key K_0 with AES by using another secret key K as the AES key. Let's assume that the attacker has no way to verify whether or not they got the valid K_0. In this case, even if the attacker could try all possible values of K, they would have no way of identifying the correct value of K, because they'd have no way of identifying the K_0 that they're after.

INT-CTXT

Integrity of ciphertexts. The security notion, applicable to authenticated encryption schemes, that it should be practically impossible for an attacker to create a valid ciphertext, even if they know many valid ciphertexts for messages of their choice.

A related theorem: if an authenticated cipher is IND-CPA and INT-CTXT, it's also IND-CCA. I leave it to you to Google the proof for this result.

Invisible signature

A public-key signature that cannot be identified as valid or invalid unless the signer has agreed to reveal that information. An invisible signature might appear to make the signature anonymous (that is, because the signature doesn't reveal the signer's identity or public key), but this isn't necessarily the case. Consider this counterexample: if you additionally sign the signature with a noninvisible signature scheme, the scheme remains invisible but is clearly not anonymous.

🔒 See *Anonymous signature, Undeniable signature.*

IOTA

By its own definition, a blockchain with no blocks and no chain. Probably the most mocked blockchain platform, because it has made some unfortunate cryptographic choices, such as designing a new hash function.

Cryptography enthusiasts and IOTA supporters have posted hundreds of inflammatory tweets about IOTA's questionable design choices. Here is a very brief summary of the debate: the crypto enthusiasts yelled, "IOTA is broken because its signature scheme is broken." In response, IOTA fans responded, "IOTA isn't broken because it can't be exploited." There is some truth to both sides.

IPES (Improved Proposed Encryption Standard)

An alternative name for the IDEA block cipher.

🔒 See *IDEA.*

IPSec

One of the major open secure channel protocols along with TLS and SSH. Despite its widespread use, it remains much less known in the cryptography community and among engineers. Indeed, you don't need to understand IPSec if you're developing mobile or web applications. Also, its design and subprotocols look cryptographically boring. A product of DARPA- and NSA-sponsored efforts that began in the 1970s, IPSec nonetheless remains the standard for network layer security. In addition, its design and implementations have proven more robust than early SSL and TLS versions except for the weak IKEv1 subprotocol.

ISO standard

Buy this definition for $180. Please note that a paper format is currently unavailable.

Isogeny-based cryptography

The youngest class of post-quantum cryptography methods; initiated in the early 2000s. An isogeny is a function that maps points of an elliptic curve to points of another elliptic curve and that satisfies specific mathematical properties. You can then draw a graph whose nodes are elliptic curves and whose edges are isogenies between them, and walk through this graph in a pseudorandom way. After throwing a lot of cool math at the study of these objects—graph theory, quaternion algebras, and so on—you end up with hard computational problems that you can use for crypto applications.

Journal of Cryptology (JoC)

Cryptography's *Nature* minus the publication fees.

KASUMI

A variant of the 1995 block cipher MISTY1; used in 3G telecommunications standards as the A5/3 cipher. KASUMI is broken, because a practical key-recovery attack exists. KASUMI is also not broken, because said attack requires chosen-ciphertext queries in the related-key model, which isn't realistic.

Keccak

The hash function family standardized as SHA-3; it is built from a single permutation according to the sponge function framework. Keccak's permutation performs a clever combination of XORs and logical ANDs. It's also optimized for efficiency and easily scales to different widths.

The original Keccak design and its sponge mode have led to several other algorithms.

🔒 See *Permutation-based cryptography.*

KeeLoq

The most expensive broken cipher ever. One of the rare block ciphers to rely on a feedback shift register.

KEM (key encapsulation mechanism)

A public-key encryption scheme designed to encrypt and decrypt short, fixed-size chunks of data; commonly used to encapsulate a symmetric key. You can think of a KEM as a key agreement in which one party gets to choose the key; a KEM's encryption function picks a random symmetric key and encrypts it, whereas the KEM's decryption function decrypts it to recover the symmetric key. It can then continue to decrypt any data encrypted using that key with some symmetric primitives.

Kerberos

The ancestor of single sign-on systems, designed in the late 1980s to provide secure authentication and authorization to MIT's distributed computing platform Athena. Admittedly an elder technology, Kerberos is one of the security protocols that relatively few people know despite its major impact and the fact that it's still used in many places, such as in the Radius authentication protocol. Indeed, in spite of its old age, Kerberos remains a decently secure protocol. It implements often forgotten concepts, such as not trusting any party until they're authenticated and not exposing passwords in clear. It has some limitations; for instance, Kerberos must rely on a trusted third party. But then again, how many security protocols ultimately don't? Sometimes known as a protocol that uses only symmetric cryptography, Kerberos can also support public-key crypto, as well as various authentication forms, such as one-time passwords, hardware tokens, and biometrics.

HADES' DOG

The origin of the Kerberos protocol's name is best explained by the goddess Athena in her conversation with Euripides (as reproduced on MIT's Kerberos site):

Euripides: (. . .) You know, I think we have a solid basis on which to implement the Charon Authentication System.

Athena: Perhaps. Anyway, I don't like the name Charon.

Euripides: You don't? Since when?

Athena: I've never liked it, because the name doesn't make sense. I was talking to my Uncle Hades about it the other day, and he suggested another name, the name of his three-headed watchdog.

Euripides: Oh, you mean Cerberus.

Athena: Bite your tongue Rip! Cerberus indeed . . .

Euripides: Er, isn't that the name?

Athena: Yeah, if you happen to be a Roman! I'm a Greek goddess, he's a Greek watchdog, and his name is Kerberos, Kerberos with a K.

Euripides: Okay, okay, don't throw thunderbolts. I'll buy the name. Actually, it has a nice ring to it. Adios Charon and hello to Kerberos.

Kerckhoffs' principles

The six principles, or *desiderata*, of security established by the 19th-century Dutch cryptographer Auguste Kerckhoffs in his article "La cryptographie militaire" (in French).

Of the six principles in Kerckhoffs' paper, only the second is commonly known as *Kerckhoffs' principle*. But all six deserve our attention. Let's examine them here:

1. *The system must be practically, if not mathematically, indecipherable.* Today's equivalent would also include systems that are virtually indecipherable by mathematical means, as when security proofs guarantee practical security under some hardness assumptions.

2. *It must not be required to be secret, and it must be able to fall into the hands of the enemy without inconvenience.* All serious cryptographers should follow this . . . except when they shouldn't. Indeed, in rare exceptions, making the algorithm secret (via custom design, secret S-boxes, secret tweak input, and/or secret personalization values) contributes significantly to the security of a system.

3. *Its key must be communicable and retainable without the help of written notes, and changeable or modifiable at the will of the correspondents.* Key distribution, revocation, and rotation remain among the most challenging problems in cryptography, and the source of many perils.

4. *It must be applicable to telegraphic correspondence.* Sorry, Kerckhoffs; the problem of email encryption is still practically unsolved.

5. *Apparatus and documents must be portable, and its usage and function must not require the concourse of several people.* This goal is the opposite of that of protocols, such as distributed key generation and threshold encryption.

6. *Finally, it is necessary, given the circumstances that command its application, that the system be easy to use, requiring neither mental strain nor the knowledge of a long series of rules to observe.* Simplicity has rarely been a major concern in cryptographic designs, although it ought to be.

Key derivation function (KDF)

A function that hashes stuff to obtain a key. A simple hash function doesn't always do the trick, because the *stuff* to be hashed typically includes a combination of secret and nonsecret values. A KDF's interface helps process these values securely to avoid collisions between different sets of stuff. There is another reason hash functions aren't sufficient: a KDF must often generate keys of arbitrary size, whereas most hash functions generate values of a fixed size.

A special case arises whenever the key can't be just any string of bits (as in the case of a symmetric key) but a public/private key pair. In those situations, rather than generating the key pair as part of the KDF, you would generally use a second algorithm to deterministically create a key pair from a seed.

Last but not least, when the stuff's secret is a password, passphrase, or other low-entropy value, you need a special kind of KDF, called a *password hash function*. These have some additional security requirements.

🔒 See *Password hash function.*

Key escrow

The idea of entrusting an organization or entity with the custody of secret keys and therefore the rights associated with them, for example, to decrypt communications.

As told by the European Council in a meeting in May 1998:

> The Council Resolution of 17 January 1995 recognised that lawfully authorised interception of communications is an important tool for the investigation of serious crime. The Council notes that law enforcement agencies may require lawful access to encryption keys, without the knowledge of the user of the cryptographic service, in order to maintain this capability. To this end, the Council recognises that one possible approach amongst others, which might meet law enforcement interests, might be the promotion of confidentiality services which involve the depositing of an encryption key or other information with a third party. Such services are often known as "key escrow" or "key recovery" services. Law enforcement agencies may also require lawful access to encryption keys where it is necessary to decrypt material which has been seized as part of a criminal investigation.

In principle, key escrow sounds easy and a fair solution to real problems. But in practice, key escrow raises a lot of procedural, technological, and political problems, and its benefits might not be worth the additional cost and risks, depending on your metric.

🔒 See *Key management.*

Key management

The single hardest problem in cryptography. Key management won't be solved by quantum computers or with an NP oracle.

Key wrapping

To symmetric cryptography, what KEMs are to public-key cryptography.

Kleptography

A term coined to refer to cryptography used in malware and other unholy applications, particularly when their aim is to steal information in a covert way; for example, via subliminal channels or obfuscation.

🔒 See *Cryptovirology.*

Known-key attack

An adversarial model that assumes the attacker already knows the secret key of some symmetric cipher. Therefore, the attack's goal isn't to recover a key but to identify structural properties that the attacker might exploit when the cipher is used in a hash function or some other construction where its key might not be secret.

Купуna (Купина)

The Ukrainian national hash function standard; established in 2014 and named after the plant *Polygonatum multiflorum*. Kupyna is based on a fairly unusual compression function construction: given a message block M and an initial hash value H, the next hash value is computed as $H \oplus \mathrm{Perm}_1(M) \oplus \mathrm{Perm}_2(M \oplus H)$, where Perm_1 and Perm_2 are permutations similar to AES with no key and a wider state.

Laconic zero-knowledge proof

An interactive proof protocol where the prover sends very few bits to the verifier.

Lai-Massey

A secure way to build a block cipher, although much less common than the Feistel substitution-permutation networks. The Lai–Massey construction is notably used by IDEA and FOX.

Given a function $f()$ whose input and output is of a length twice as short as the block size, a Lai-Massey round applies to an internal state split in two halves, L and R. Each round updates these halves as follows:

First, compute $X = f(L - R)$. Then set $L = \sigma(L + X)$ and $R = R + X$.

Here, $\sigma()$ is an orthomorphism, that is, a permutation so that the mapping $Y \mapsto \sigma(Y) - Y$ is also a permutation. For example, FOX's orthomorphism sees L as two halves $L = L_L \| L_R$ and returns $L_R \| (L_L \oplus L_R)$.

Without $\sigma()$, the difference $L - R$ remains the same through the round operation, slightly reducing the scheme's security (I'll leave the proof for this as a simple exercise for you to complete).

Lamport signature

The first hash-based signature scheme, and in its original form, the simplest signature scheme ever: to sign a one-bit message, you'd first generate a private key composed of two random values K_0 and K_1. Then you'd share the public key $(\text{Hash}(K_0), \text{Hash}(K_1))$. To sign the message 0, you'd attach K_0 as a signature, and you'd attach K_1 otherwise.

This works, but it's not very useful, because 1) a key pair can sign only one message, and 2) the key size is proportional to that of the message.

THE FIRST PUBLIC-KEY SIGNATURE SCHEME?

Although published in 1979—after the Diffie-Hellman and RSA papers—Lamport's scheme might have been the signature scheme to use public-key cryptography. In Lamport's own words:

> At a coffee house in Berkeley around 1975, Whitfield Diffie described a problem to me that he had been trying to solve: constructing a digital signature for a document. I immediately proposed a solution. Though not very practical—it required perhaps 64 bits of published key to sign a single bit—it was the first digital signature algorithm.

Lattice-based cryptography

The most promising class of post-quantum cryptography schemes, as far as real applications are concerned. Lattice-based cryptography usually relies on some version of the learning with errors (LWE) problem and in particular its relation to lattice problems. It can provide encryption/KEM and signature schemes. It's generally considered the most promising type of post-quantum scheme due to its combination of acceptable security assurance, performance, and diversity of constructions.

Lattice-based schemes represent 39 percent of round one submissions to NIST's post-quantum competition, 46 percent of submissions selected in round two, and 71 percent of the finalists.

🔒 See *Learning with errors (LWE)*.

Le Chiffre

A character in an Ian Fleming spy book. Anyone whose name means *The Cipher* can only be a villain:

> Mostly expensive, but discreet. Large sexual appetites. Flagellant. Expert driver of fast cars. Adept with small arms and other forms of personal combat, including knives. Carries three Eversharp razor blades, in hatband, heel of left shoe, and cigarette case. Knowledge of accountancy and mathematics. Fine gambler.

Leakage-resilient cryptography

An attempt to model side-channel information leaks using abstract models of computation and memory leakage. Such models include the Bounded Retrieval Model, Continual Memory Leakage, Auxiliary Memory Leakage, and Only Computation Leaks, among others. Building secure schemes within these models has proved an interesting exercise, yet of questionable practical interest, because the models largely fail to capture the complex reality of side channels and physical attacks.

Learning with errors (LWE)

The problem of solving a system of linear equations when the equations have errors in them. LWE generalizes the *learning parity with noise* (LPN) problem so it has arbitrary dimensions and numbers greater than 0 and 1.

Lattice-based cryptography schemes often rely on the hardness of some LWE problem. The reason is that, on average, LWE is as hard as the hardest instances of a lattice problem, such as GapSVP. The resulting cryptographic constructions should be, in turn, at least as hard to break as LWE.

Length extension attack

The property of certain hash functions that given Hash(X), and without knowing X, it's trivial to find the value of Hash($X \| \text{pad} \| Y$) for any Y, where pad is padding bits followed by the encoding of X's length. Hash functions vulnerable to length extension include all those built with the Merkle–Damgård construction, such as SHA-256 and RIPEMD-160. More recent hash functions, such as SHA-3 or BLAKE3, aren't vulnerable to length extension.

Length-preserving encryption

Encryption that creates ciphertexts of exactly the same bit size as their corresponding plaintext; for example, encrypting any 16-byte plaintext into a 16-byte ciphertext, any 1-byte plaintext into a 1-byte ciphertext, any 2-bit plaintext into a 2-bit ciphertext, and so on. In applications where the payload length is fixed, length-preserving encryption is necessary to encrypt payload data.

Length-preserving encryption shouldn't be confused with *format-preserving encryption*.

PRESERVING PLAINTEXT LENGTH

Length-preserving encryption might sound simple, but it's not. First, public-key encryption schemes cannot directly offer length-preserving encryption, because ciphertext expansion is intrinsic to how they work. For example, RSA encryption requires additional padding and randomness to achieve secure encryption (IND-CPA).

When it comes to symmetric encryption, the only way to achieve IND-CPA-secure length-preserving encryption is if the nonce or IV is not seen as a part of the ciphertext.

Stream ciphers are trivially length-preserving, because they XOR pseudo-random bits with the plaintext and thus preserve its length through encryption. Likewise, the CTR-mode creates ciphertexts of identical length as their plaintext.

What about a block cipher mode like CBC? If you use the standard PKCS#7 padding scheme, the ciphertext will inevitably be longer than the plaintext. But there's a technique called *ciphertext stealing* that shuffles the bytes in the last blocks to obtain a ciphertext of the same length as its plaintext.

LFSR (linear feedback shift register)

🔒 See *Feedback shift register.*

Lightweight cryptography

Cryptography optimized for IoT devices and other platforms that have memory and logic constraints. But these constrained platforms usually have unique limitations and therefore require unique designs. Consequently, academic research about lightweight cryptography has been of disappointing practical relevance, sometimes because embedded platforms often include an AES logic.

Linear cryptanalysis

A cryptanalysis technique for symmetric ciphers that exploits patterns described in terms of linear equations, or equations consisting only of XORs between bits.

Linear cryptanalysis might look totally different from differential cryptanalysis, but it's actually closely related to it. The most successful linear attack is arguably the one on DES.

Linkability

A property of a signature scheme that allows an attacker to determine whether two signatures were issued by the same signer. Of course, standard signatures, such as ECDSA signatures, are linkable by design, which is fine. But nonlinkability is a requirement for ring signatures.

LM hash

Short for LAN Manager hash, the function that hashes users' passwords in earlier Microsoft Windows versions. LM hash is the predecessor of NT hash, which is a stronger hash.

🔒 See *NT hash.*

In hindsight, LM hash is laughably weak: it's barely a hash because you can recover the original passwords very easily.

To hash a password with LM hash, follow these steps:

1. Convert lowercase letters to uppercase letters. This makes collisions frequent, which is bad, while also making the recovery of the initial password informationally impossible, a fact probably not intended as a security feature.

2. If the password is longer than 14 characters, truncate it to its first 14 characters (another way to create trivial collisions); otherwise, pad it with null bytes to get a 14-byte string.

3. Encrypt the string *KGS!@#$%* using two DES instances, one with the first seven bytes of the padded password and another with the last seven bytes (remember that DES's key is 56 bits long).

4. The hash is the concatenation of two ciphertexts!

Luby-Rackoff

🔒 See *Feistel network.*

Lucifer

The block cipher designed by Horst Feistel at IBM that led to the DES standard. It wasn't originally a Feistel network, but a substitution-permutation network like AES, with blocks of 32, 48, or 128 bits. Lucifer was initially implemented in APL (A Programming Language) and code-named *Demonstration*. But the APL workspace restricted projects' name length, so *Demonstration* became *Demon* and later *Lucifer.*

MAC (message authentication code)

Not a signature, but very close: like a public-key signature a MAC should be unforgeable without the key, but unlike a public-key signature a MAC doesn't provide nonrepudiation.

In theory, a MAC can be unforgeable yet leak information about the message, but in practice most MACs don't.

MAGENTA

An unfortunate candidate at the AES competition, broken literally minutes after it was presented at the first AES conference. A conference participant commented: "It got so bad that a few of the participants started doing real-time cryptanalysis and suggesting attacks that would break the algorithm right there and then. I marvelled that the German guy managed to keep his composure. The whole spectacle was rather shameful."

Malleability

An underappreciated security notion: an encryption scheme is nonmalleable if an attacker cannot turn a ciphertext Enc(K, M) into another valid ciphertext Enc(K, $f(M)$) for some specified function $f()$. A nonmalleable scheme is therefore more secure than a malleable one. In the chosen-ciphertext model, nonmalleability is equivalent to indistinguishability (the strongest security notion).

Manger attack

A padding oracle attack on RSA encryption in OAEP mode. The Manger attack is less well known than the Bleichenbacher attack on older RSA encryption, because it's generally harder to exploit. Indeed, as Manger's original paper noted, the PKCS standard already described a partial mitigation against his attack when saying that "it is important that the error messages output in steps 4 [integer-to-octets conversion] and 5 [OAEP decoding] be the same." But as with Bleichenbacher's attack, Manger's attack also works if the attacker exploits timing leaks instead of error messages.

Man-in-the-middle

A class of attacks where the attacker surreptitiously captures and modifies traffic from two or more correspondents. The FREAK (Factoring RSA Export Keys) attack on TLS implementations is an example of a man-in-the-middle attack in which the attacker modifies session initiation data to force the use of a weak cipher suite.

🔒 See *Meet-in-the-middle*.

MASH (Modular Arithmetic Secure Hash)

An early attempt at a hash function relying on the same operations as RSA.

🔒 See *VSH (Very Smooth Hash)*.

McEliece encryption scheme

🔒 See *Code-based cryptography*.

MD4

Hash function even weaker than MD5.

MD5

Previously a synonym of *checksum* and *hash function*, now a sign of poor cryptography design because it isn't collision resistant. But MD5 is still secure against preimage attacks.

MDC (Message Digest Cipher)

Old-fashioned name for hash functions.

MDC-2 (Modification Detection Code 2)

A construction that turns an n-bit block cipher into a hash function with $2n$-bit output. The resulting hash is less secure than an ideal $2n$-bit hash but more secure than an n-bit hash. MDC-2 was mainly used with DES as *MDC-2DES* except when IBM's patent was a concern.

Meet-in-the-middle

A folklore cryptanalysis technique mainly known for its application in attacking symmetric primitives. A meet-in-the-middle is applicable when consecutive encryption layers (also called *rounds* or *cipher instances*) work with independent keys. For example, when encrypting a message M as $C = \text{Enc}^2(K_2, \text{Enc}^1(K_1, M))$ with two n-bit keys K_1 and K_2 and two distinct ciphers Enc^1 and Enc^2, you might expect a security of $2n$ bits (as if it were equivalent to encrypting with a $2n$-bit key). But the actual security is closer to n bits: the reason is that, given a pair (C, M)

you can compute $X = \mathrm{Dec}^2(K, C)$ for all the 2^n values of K, and then compute $Y = \mathrm{Enc}^1(K', M)$ for all 2^n values of K'. The pair (K', K) for which $X = Y$ is then likely to be (K_1, K_2).

You can view this trick as one instance of a more general optimization technique found in many cryptanalytic attacks. Those attacks include the baby-step giant-step algorithm (to compute discrete logarithms), the GHS isogeny-based attack on ECDLP, or attacks on isogeny-based schemes.

🔒 See *Man-in-the-middle*.

Merkle puzzle

The closest thing to public-key cryptography before (secure) public-key cryptography was invented.

Merkle tree

A solution to many problems in cryptography and computing. Essentially, a hash tree. It can, for example, be used to demonstrate the knowledge of some large set of data in a compact and efficient way: you can prove that a piece of data is in the tree by showing the list of nodes required to compute the root node from the said data's node (usually a leaf). This list of values has been called the *authentication path*, *inclusion proof*, and *Merkle proof*.

Merkle trees are the main components of hash-based signatures.

Merkle–Damgård construction

A straightforward technique for hashing messages of any length when using a hash function that hashes only short messages. It does this in such a way that, if the short-length hash is secure, the resulting hash of any length is secure as well. This is one of the earliest security proofs in symmetric cryptography. But this proof is only about collision resistance and preimage resistance, not about security in the most absolute sense. For example, Merkle–Damgård hash functions, such as SHA-256, are vulnerable to length extension attacks.

Mersenne twister

Not a cryptographic pseudorandom generator.

Message franking

A protocol to allow the reporting of abusive messages in an end-to-end encryption conversation while maintaining an acceptable level of security. Motivated by Facebook's problem of deploying end-to-end encryption in Messenger, yet with the possibility of users to report messages to Facebook in a way that their sender can't cryptographically deny their sending. Therefore, it requires quite the opposite of plausible deniability.

Miller–Rabin

The most common probabilistic primality test. Under certain conditions, you can fool the test into declaring that a composite number is prime.

🔓 See *PRIMES*.

MINERVA

🔓 See *Crypto AG*.

Mining

Hashing for money.

Misuse resistance

Defense-in-depth applied to cryptography. Misuse resistance counters the fact that some ciphers, such as AES-GCM, are secure only if you never call them twice with the same nonce. (A nonce is the auxiliary input that ensures that you'll get a different ciphertext if you encrypt the same plaintext twice with the same key.) Misuse-resistant ciphers attempt to eliminate this problem. Their only limitation is that if you encrypt the same message with the same key and nonce twice, the output will be the same. (As an exercise, find why this limitation can't be avoided.) The only security flaw is that an attacker will learn when you've encrypted the same message twice. SIV-AES is an example of such a cipher.

Misuse resistance can extend to cases other than symmetric encryption. It also applies to APIs to prevent disasters when the caller forgets to read the documentation (if it exists).

In the case of AES-GCM, reusing a nonce allows an attacker to learn the XOR difference between the two plaintext messages, even if they don't know either of the messages. Proof: AES-GCM encrypts a message by using the CTR (counter) mode, which, given a key and a nonce, generates a pseudo-random sequence, called the *keystream*, XORed to the message. So if you generate the keystream S and create the ciphertext $C_1 = M_1 \oplus S$ from the message M_1 by reusing the same key and nonce, you'll also use the same S to encrypt a second message M_2 to $C_2 = M_2 \oplus S$. In that case, an attacker can compute $C_1 \oplus C_2 = M_1 \oplus M_2$. This is bad. QED.

Mixnet

A multi-party protocol that provides anonymity by shuffling a sequence of ciphertexts $C_1, \ldots, C_n$ into another sequence $C'_1, \ldots, C'_n$, so that for each C_i there exists a C'_j whose value is distinct but decrypts to the same plaintext. The protocol might also include a zero-knowledge proof that shows that the criterion is satisfied without leaking any information about the permutation or plaintexts.

Most often, mixnets are used to route data in anonymous communication networks. Here, an observer shouldn't be able to associate a post-mix value C'_i to its pre-mix counterpart C_j. After one or more rounds of mixing, this prevents an attacker from associating a message's source with its final recipient.

Mixnets were also used in e-voting schemes to provide voter anonymity, as well as in cryptocurrencies to hide sender/recipient relations, typically by shuffling UTXOs.

A number of gotchas can defeat mixnets' security. For example, in the case of anonymous routing, the mixing router must transmit the mixed values in an order not correlated with that of received values; otherwise, anonymity can be easily compromised. Messages should also all be of the same size; otherwise, the permutation is straightforward to identify.

MQV (Menezes-Qu-Vanstone)

Diffie–Hellman on steroids. Invented in 1995, yet rarely used, in part because of patents covering it. It's the sister of HMQV and ECMQV (once in NSA's Suite B). Today, MQV is perhaps best known for its use in the password-based key agreement protocol OPAQUE.

Multicollision

For hash functions, a collision between more than two messages. It takes less time to find multicollisions on iterated hash functions (such as SHA-256) than for a hash function accessed as a black box. If intermediate chaining values of the iterated hash are n-bit, then a k-collision can be found in $\lceil \log_2 k \rceil \cdot 2^{n/2}$ against $k!^{1/k} \cdot 2^{n(k-1)/k}$ for an ideal, black-box hash.

Multi-party computation (MPC)

A class of cryptographic techniques for computing a function's output without knowing the inputs' original values. MPC is a rich field of research, yet with few major application until cryptocurrency wallets, which also use the MPC-like threshold signatures. Many more real-world MPC applications are expected.

Multivariate cryptography

A class of post-quantum schemes based on the hardness of solving systems of nonlinear equations in multiple variables. The hardness of such problems is related to that of Multivariate Quadratics (MQ), the problem of solving a random system of degree-2 equations, known to be NP-complete.

Most multivariate schemes are signature schemes that produce short signatures (good) but require long public keys (not so good).

NBS (National Bureau of Standards)

Previous name for NIST.

🔒 See *NIST (National Institute of Standards and Technology)*.

NESSIE (New European Schemes for Signatures, Integrity, and Encryption)

A project that ran from 2000 to 2003 and was headed by seven European institutions. It selected 17 recommended algorithms among 42 submissions.

NESSIE's selected algorithms didn't become formal standards, only informal recommendations, which in hindsight drew little interest: does anyone remember ACE Encrypt, SHACAL-2, or SFLASH?

"New Directions in Cryptography"

Invited research paper published in IEEE Transactions on Information Theory in November 1976, by Whitfield Diffie and Martin Hellman. Today, the Diffie–Hellman operation is used in almost every software or hardware system that performs cryptographic operations.

THE DIFFIE-HELLMAN REVOLUTION

Diffie and Hellman can non-ironically be called visionaries after writing the following introduction:

> We stand today on the brink of a revolution in cryptography. The development of cheap digital hardware has freed it from the design limitations of mechanical computing and brought the cost of high grade cryptographic devices down to where they can be used in such commercial applications as remote cash dispensers and computer terminals. In turn, such applications create a need for new types of cryptographic systems which minimize the necessity of secure key distribution channels and supply the equivalent of a written signature. At the same time, theoretical developments in information theory and computer science show promise of providing provably secure cryptosystems, changing this ancient art into a science.

The paper goes on to introduce the concept of public-key cryptography, and a new *public-key distribution system*, now referred to as the Diffie–Hellman key agreement. The original specification is worth copying verbatim:

> Each user generates an independent random number X_i chosen uniformly from the set of integers $\{1, 2, \cdots, q - 1\}$. Each keeps X_i secret, but places

$$Y_i = \alpha^{X_i} \bmod q$$

in a public file with his name and address. When users i and j wish to communicate privately, they use

$$K_{ij} = \alpha^{X_i X_j} \bmod q$$

as their key. User i obtains K_{ij} by obtaining Y_j from the public file and letting

$$K_{ij} = Y_j^{X_i} \bmod q = \left(\alpha^{X_j}\right)^{X_i} \bmod q = \alpha^{X_i X_j} \bmod q$$

User j obtains K_{ij} in a similar fashion

$$K_{ij} = Y_i^{X_j} \bmod q$$

Another user must compute K_{ij} from Y_i and Y_j, for example, by computing

$$K_{ij} = Y_i^{\log_\alpha Y_j} \bmod q$$

We thus see that if logs mod q are easily computed, the system can be broken. While we do not currently have a proof of the converse (i.e., that the system is secure if logs mod q are difficult to compute), neither do we see any way to compute K_{ij} from Y_i and Y_j without first obtaining either X_i or X_j.

After discussing signatures (as *one-way authentication*) and computational complexity, the paper concludes,

We hope this will inspire others to work in this fascinating area in which participation has been discouraged in the recent past by a nearly total government monopoly.

It certainly did.

NFSR (nonlinear feedback shift register)

🔒 See *Feedback shift register*.

NIST (National Institute of Standards and Technology)

The agency responsible for US Federal standards in various technical fields, including cryptography. NIST cryptography standards and recommendations have included algorithms (such as DSS, AES, SHA-2, SHA-3, and so on), block cipher operation modes, SHA-3 variants (such as cSHAKE, KMAC, and TupleHash), key management, random generation, and statistical tests.

The design of NIST-standardized algorithms, such as AES and SHA-3, was crowdsourced to cryptographers from all around the world through a public, transparent process. This approach is believed to be more reliable than delegating cryptographic algorithms design to NSA.

NIZK (non-interactive zero-knowledge)

A NIZK proof is a zero-knowledge proof that comes as a single message, as opposed to an interactive protocol involving multiple messages between a prover and a verifier. NIZK proofs often use the Fiat–Shamir heuristic to turn an interactive protocol into a noninteractive one.

Noekeon

A block cipher with a rare property: the encryption algorithm is the same as the decryption algorithm. This is convenient in environments with limited code, silicon, or developer time.

Noise

A framework for designing protocols using the Diffie–Hellman protocol. A Noise protocol can sometimes (but not always) replace TLS to implement transport security. This offers multiple potential benefits, including greater simplicity, identity hiding, and lower bandwidth usage.

Nonce

In the context of cryptography, a *number used only once*. An additional input to some cryptographic operation whose value should always be unique. This ensures that the operation will always produce different outputs, even if all inputs are identical. In practice, guaranteeing nonce uniqueness isn't always straightforward, and nonces are typically generated at random. Authenticated ciphers will usually use a nonce to ensure that if you encrypt the same message twice, the output ciphertext will look different, thereby preventing an attacker from noticing that the same message was encrypted again.

Non-committing encryption

Sounds like deniable encryption, but not necessarily deniable. Using non-committing encryption, a fake ciphertext can be created in such a way that it looks like a real one. It can be shown to have been created from any plaintext by revealing a key pair and random bits that connect the ciphertext to the plaintext.

Non-outsourceability

A property of a proof-of-work scheme whose work cannot be out-sourced without revealing the private key of the prover. So it prevents pooled mining, where third parties perform a share of the work and are supposed to get a share of the mining reward. Such a proof must be efficiently verifiable without the private key.

Non-slanderability

In the context of ring signatures, a security property that prevents an attacker from forging a valid signature that can be linked to a specific member of the group of authorized signers. Although expressed in slightly different terms, non-slanderability is equivalent to unforgeability.

NSA (National Security Agency)

Cryptographers' favorite three-letter agency. The NSA employs many cryptographers but never publishes in peer-reviewed conferences. However, it's active in cryptography research, having designed established public standards (such as DSA, SHA-2, and the unfortunate Dual_EC_DRBG), unclassified candidate standards (the block ciphers SIMON and SPECK), declassified systems (the Fortezza crypto card, including the Skipjack block cipher), and many classified algorithms. The NSA's cryptanalysis capabilities remain largely undocumented.

🔓 See *Suite A*.

NT hash

Colloquially known as NTLM hash, the password hash function used in MS Windows' NT LAN Manager (NTLM) protocol suite, and an upgrade from the legacy LAN Manager protocol. NT hash is just an MD4 hash of the encoded user password. It's better than LM hash but is also easily cracked.

🔒 See *LM hash*.

NTRU (*N*th degree Truncated polynomial Ring Units)

One of the first lattice-based cryptosystems, designed in 1996. Understudied for many years, perhaps because it was patented and commercialized.

Renewed interest in NTRU culminated in the 2016 design of NTRU Prime, an NTRU variant succinctly defined by its authors as "an efficient implementation of high-security prime-degree large-Galois-group inert-modulus ideal-lattice-based cryptography," where "*Prime degree* etc. are three features that (. . .) take various mathematical tools away from the attacker." NTRU Prime was submitted to NIST's post-quantum competition.

Null cipher

A term that means *no encryption* when encountered as a cipher suite. For example, early TLS versions supported the null cipher. The null cipher needs no key, and I suppose you could consider it the fastest cipher.

OAEP (Optimal Asymmetric Encryption Padding)

Method for securely padding a message before public-key encryption with RSA or Rabin's schemes. Computing m^e mod n is indeed not a very safe way to use the RSA operation to encrypt a message m. Instead, OAEP can convert the message into a randomized string that breaks plain RSA's malleability and homomorphicity. RSA-OAEP is now the recommended way to encrypt with RSA, following the PKCS#1 v2.2 standard.

🔒 See *All-or-nothing transform (AONT)*, *Manger attack*.

Oblivious key management system (OKMS)

Service that holds master keys and interacts with clients to derive keys without knowing said keys due to (partially) oblivious PRFs used for key derivation.

Oblivious PRF (OPRF)

A two-party protocol where a server knows the key K and a client computes $PRF(K, X)$ for some X without learning K by interacting with the server, which must learn nothing about X or $PRF(K, X)$.

Partially oblivious PRFs (pOPRFs) are a variant wherein the server can supply an additional nonsecret input.

Oblivious RAM (ORAM)

An abstract model of secure memory, designed so an attacker learns nothing when they observe the content and access patterns of the memory a program uses. In particular, they shouldn't learn what piece of data is being accessed or (to some extent) whether the access is a read or a modification of the stored data. In theory, an ORAM deals with actual RAM—as in memory a program uses—but in practice is more about ROM, a filesystem, or a database.

Oblivious transfer

A protocol to transfer data between two parties, where the receiver chooses which piece of data they want to receive among a multitude of pieces, but the sender doesn't know which piece it is.

Imagine you want to buy and download an ebook from the No Starch Press online store but don't want the publisher, Bill, to know which book you purchased. Normally, your ebook purchase request would ultimately lead to a query to No Starch's database, a file transfer from some storage media to No Starch's ebook service, and then to your device. The publisher could therefore find out which book you bought by monitoring the disk activity, database queries, file transfers, and so on.

Oblivious transfer prevents anyone from finding out which file was accessed, even if they monitored the precise data read from the storage medium. In addition, oblivious transfer guarantees to No Starch Press that you're retrieving only one book, and that you're not collecting information about others (the main feature that makes oblivious transfer different than private information retrieval).

Obscurity

A heresy for cryptographers. But in reality, when cryptography is just a part of a broader security system, you sometimes need to obscure its logic to meet your security goals.

OCB (offset codebook mode)

One of the simplest and most efficient authenticated encryption modes for block ciphers and a demonstration of cryptography's fragility. Attackers managed to break OCB2, the second version of OCB, in spite of security proofs and standardization. OCB1 and OCB3, although very similar, seem to be secure.

One-time pad

Often described as the paragon of encryption, or the perfect cipher, because it's mathematically proven to be absolutely secure. But the one-time pad used on its own is actually a weak cipher: it's trivially malleable, unauthenticated, and not misuse resistant.

One-way function

The cornerstone of modern cryptography. Easy to compute but hard to invert: a function $f()$ is one-way if, given $f(x)$ for a random unknown input x, finding a value y so that $f(y) = f(x)$ is computationally hard. (The formal definition is more rigorous than this.)

You can construct most cryptographic primitives if all you have is a one-way function; in practice, many functions in cryptography, such as hash functions, appear to be one-way. But in theory, we have no proof that one-way functions actually exist. In fact, the existence of one-way functions implies $P \neq NP$ (the proof is left as an exercise for you to complete).

Onion-AE

The notion of strong authenticated encryption in the context of Tor's onion routing. In onion-AE encryption, the authenticity of a message must only be checked at the last (exit) node, yet covers the entire route of the message, from its initial sender.

OPAQUE

Pronounced O-PAKE. The O represents oblivious PRF, the most interesting part of the OPAQUE password-authenticated key agreement (PAKE). It allows the client to compute the hash of a combination of two values when it knows only one of the two (its password).

There are some caveats: although authentication is about proving knowledge of a password, the client also needs a traditional public-key pair and must therefore protect its private key. Also, to get a full PAKE with secure shared key agreement, it must be combined with another protocol, such as HMQV.

🔒 See *Oblivious PRF (OPRF)*.

OpenSSL

One of the most important pieces of cryptographic software. Foremost a command line utility that supports a multitude of cryptographic operations (key generation, signature, encryption, certificate creation, encoding/decoding of various formats, and so on) for a multitude of algorithms (block ciphers, hash functions, elliptic curves, and so on, as well as legacy algorithms) and their parameters, and that runs on numerous CPU types and operating systems.

If that isn't enough, OpenSSL also provides two libraries: a cryptographic library (libcrypto) and an implementation of the SSL and TLS protocols (libssl), which uses libcrypto.

OPENSSL'S KITCHEN

OpenSSL is like a 24/7 restaurant that offers burgers and pizza, as well as Japanese sushi, French coq au vin, Mexican tacos, and Swiss fondue. It's extremely difficult to serve all dishes with the same level of quality.

It also means that the kitchen must be a real mess. As cryptography professor Matthew Green once said,

> OpenSSL is the space shuttle of crypto libraries. It will get you to space, provided you have a team of people to push the ten thousand buttons required to do so.

Oracle

Rather like a crystal ball, an abstract entity that will respond to your requests, which cryptographers call oracle queries.

The idea of cryptographic oracles comes from the *oracles* of complexity theory, where, for example, you attempt to solve problem 1 using an oracle that magically gives you solutions to problem 2, given the description of an instance of problem 2. Given a factoring oracle, for instance, you can break RSA.

Oracles are an abstraction used in research papers as a device to simplify security arguments, proofs, or cryptanalytic attacks. You might encounter encryption oracles, decryption oracles, factorization oracles, and many more. Random oracles are the most common because of their unique role in proofs of security.

🔒 See *Random oracle.*

OTR (Off-the-Record)

The end-to-end encryption protocol initially designed for synchronous communications. Capable of running atop messaging protocols, such as XMPP or IRC. A unique aspect of OTR is its deniability property, whereby peers can deny having sent a message by leaking the MAC key used to sign it. OTR is the basis for what became known as the Signal protocol.

Padding oracle attack

A class of side-channel attacks that exploit information about whether the padding of some encrypted message is valid. An attacker could learn that information by measuring the decryption execution time, which sometimes depends on the padding's correctness. The most common padding oracle attacks are those applied to the CBC block cipher mode, the Bleichenbacher attack on PKCS#1 v1.5, and Manger attack on OAEP (PKCS#1 v2) encryption. The idea of padding oracles can be generalized to format oracles, which reveal the existence of some known pattern in the decrypted message (for example, a specific encoding or character set).

Developers have sometimes deployed countermeasures to padding oracle attacks accidentally—namely, when certain implementations don't check the padding correctly (but this creates other problems).

🔒 See *Bleichenbacher attack, CBC (cipher block chaining), Manger attack.*

Paillier cryptosystem

A public-key encryption scheme that is a bit more mathematically interesting than RSA, ElGamal, and IES. Paillier's encryption has the rare property of additive homomorphism, meaning that $\text{Dec}(\text{Enc}(M_1) \times \text{Enc}(M_2)) = M_1 + M_2$. Its security is based on the hardness of the factoring problem as well as that of a related problem—the decisional composite residuosity problem, introduced with Paillier's cryptosystem, which is about deciding whether there exists x such that $y = x^d \bmod n^2$ given n and y.

Pairing

In public-key cryptography, nothing to do with the Bluetooth pairing operation. A pairing is a map $e()$ of two group elements to an element from another group, with the following property, for any R, S, T:

$$e(R + S, T) = e(R, T)e(S, T)$$

This is called bilinearity and is what makes pairings useful in cryptography. These properties hold as well for a bilinear pairing:

$$e(S, -T) = e(-S, T) = e(S, T)^{-1}$$
$$e(aS, bT) = e(S, T)^{ab}$$

The bilinear counterpart of the Diffie–Hellman problem for pairings is the following: given P, aP, bP, cP, find $e(P, P)^{abc}$. For well-chosen types of pairing and elliptic curves, this problem is believed to be about as hard as its classical version.

Pairing-based cryptography

Cryptography that uses pairings, duh. Pairings on elliptic curves allow the creation of bilinear maps, which allow you to construct—under some hardness assumptions—secure functionalities that classical, discrete, logarithm-based elliptic-curve cryptography cannot. These functionalities include one-round three-party key agreement, identity-based encryption, attribute-based encryption, short signatures, and verifiable random functions.

Cryptographers began using pairings in cryptography to achieve three-party key agreement in just one round of communication. With pairings, this works as follows, given a common base point P:

- Alice generates an integer a and broadcasts aP.
- Bob generates an integer b and broadcasts bP.
- Chris generates an integer c and broadcasts cP.

Then Alice computes the shared secret as $e(bP, cP)^a = e(P, P)^{abc}$. Bob and Chris run a similar operation to obtain the same value.

PAKE (password-authenticated key exchange)

An authenticated key agreement (or exchange) protocol where the client's authentication relies on the knowledge of a password. In most PAKEs, the server doesn't know the password but only some data derived from it. PAKEs where both parties know the password are called balanced PAKEs.

PAKEs try to prevent the straightforward password-guessing attacks possible in send-the-password-or-its-hash methods of key exchange. But this small benefit comes at a high cost: PAKEs add complexity and deployment cost, which is why they're rarely used. As Matthew Green wrote, "Many people don't want to run a *key exchange* protocol in the first place! They just want to verify that a user knows a password."

Paradigm

An overused word in cryptography, especially when preceded by *new*.

Password hash function

A hash function whose goal is to be slow rather than fast.

If M is an arbitrary string of bits, then given a hash value $H = \text{Hash}(M)$, you'll never find M. The reason is that 1) finding any preimage of H will be computationally infeasible if H is long enough, and 2) even with infinite computing power, you'd have no way of singling out M among all the values that map to H, which is impossible, according to the pigeon-hole principle.

But if you know that *M* is a password chosen by a human, retrieving it becomes much easier. You might be able to find a password *M* that hashes to *H* and be reasonably sure that it was the password hashed in the first place, because there are way fewer rememberable passwords than possible values of *H*. In other words, as an unknown input value, a typical password has much lower entropy than an arbitrary string.

The more you know about the person who chose the password, the easier this is, and the lower the password's entropy. For example, if you know the person is a 65-year-old woman living in Tennessee, you'll probably try a specific set of passwords; you'd try a different set if the person is a 20-year-old Swiss guy. The consequence of this is that passwords are fairly easy to find given their hash values: you just repeatedly hash possible passwords and compare the results with the given hash.

The mitigation we use is very dumb, but it works: instead of using a secure and efficient hash function, we use a function that is secure but inefficient—slow to compute and sometimes also uses large amounts of memory (which makes password cracking even more difficult when using GPUs or dedicated hardware).

PBKDF2 (Password-Based Key Derivation Function 2)

Password-based key derivation function, second version of the standard. PBKDF2 is the poor man's password hash. It's good enough in most cases when tuned with enough iterations, but it's not as cool as Argon2.

PCT (Private Communications Technology)

Microsoft's secure communication protocol. PCT competed with SSL v3 in the mid-1990s. PCT intended to address SSL v2's flaws yet be somewhat compatible with it. But only Microsoft has used it, and it was ultimately replaced by SSL v3 or TLS everywhere.

PEP (Plaintext equivalence proof)

A protocol that checks whether two ciphertexts are encryptions of the same value. Participants cannot cheat.

Perfect forward secrecy

🔓 See *Forward secrecy.*

Permutation-based cryptography

Cryptographic schemes that leverage a single permutation to provide other functionalities. It's based on research related to the Keccak hash function.

Permutation-based cryptography from the Keccak extended family includes many constructions, modes, and primitives, which we've tried to inventory in the following subdictionary:

- SHAKE, a XOF (part of the FIPS 202 standard)
- cSHAKE, variant of SHAKE (part of NIST SP 800-185)
- KMAC, a variable-length MAC (part of NIST SP 800-185)
- ParallelHash, a parallelizable XOF (part of NIST SP 800-185)
- TupleHash, a XOF designed to hash tuples of data (part of NIST SP 800-185)
- Duplex, an extension of the sponge construction
- MonkeyDuplex, a variant of Duplex to build authentication encryption schemes
- DonkeySponge, a variant of Duplex to build MACs
- Keccup, a reduced-round version of Keccak
- Ketje (and its versions Ketje Jr, Ketje Sr, Ketje Minor, and Ketje Major), a lightweight authenticated cipher
- Keyak (and its versions River, Lake, Sea, Ocean, and Lunar Keyak), an authenticated cipher
- KangarooTwelve, a fast parallel XOF
- Dec (doubly extendable cryptographic) functions
- Deck (doubly extendable cryptographic keyed) functions
- Kravatte, a deck function, coming with KravatteModes, modes on top of it
- Farfalle, a construction to build a deck function
- Cyclist, the mode of operation of Xoodyak
- Motorist, the mode of operation of Keyak
- Xoofff, a deck function, coming with XoofffModes, modes on top of it
- Xoofffie, a variant of Xoofff
- Xoodoo, a family of permutations
- Xoodyak, a lightweight scheme (performing authenticated encryption, MAC, hashing, and so on)

- Mixifer, a 256-bit permutation
- Mr. Monster Burrito, a variable-length block cipher

Most likely, this is an incomplete list of the Keccak bestiary, but gives you an idea of the creativity and innovation of the Keccak designers.

PES (Proposed Encryption Standard)

A block cipher presented at Eurocrypt 1990. It didn't become a standard.

🔒 See *IDEA, IPES.*

PET (Plaintext equivalence test)

A protocol that checks whether two ciphertexts are encryptions of the same value. But participants can cheat.

PFS

A secret advanced cryptography think tank.

🔒 See *Forward secrecy.*

PGP (Pretty Good Privacy)

The first major, public cryptography software, developed in the early 1990s. PGP later became an enterprise encryption product. Currently, pgp.com redirects to broadcom.com, because Symantec acquired the PGP company and Broadcom later acquired Symantec. The OpenPGP message format and the GnuPG (GPG) software are the open source legacies of PGP. In 2020, PGP remains the de facto standard for email encryption and is used by major enterprise and open source email encryption software.

PGP is often called broken, mostly because the 1990s design didn't anticipate security requirements of the 2010s. Also, its software implementations turned out to have security flaws—as pretty much all software does.

Photuris

The Latin name for a genus of fireflies. Also, a session-key management protocol for IPSec that is, according to *informed speculation*, similar to NSA's FIREFLY protocol (allegedly part of Suite A and used in EKMS).

🔒 See *Suite A.*

Picnic

A post-quantum signature scheme that doesn't fit in any of the established categories of post-quantum schemes. A Picnic signature proves the signer's knowledge of the key to a block cipher, given a plaintext-ciphertext pair as a public key.

Picnic achieves this by using a noninteractive proof of knowledge and a block cipher (lowMC) that lends itself to such proofs.

PKC

Officially, "The International Conference on Practice and Theory in Public Key Cryptography." The PKC conference is to public-key cryptography what FSE is to symmetric cryptography, but it covers more diverse and mathematical topics.

Researchers present peer-reviewed research papers with titles such as "Safety in Numbers: On the Need for Robust Diffie–Hellman Parameter Validation" and "Committed MPC—Maliciously Secure Multiparty Computation from Homomorphic Commitments."

🔒 See *Asiacrypt, CHES, CRYPTO, Eurocrypt, FSE, Real World Crypto, TCC.*

PKCS (Public Key Cryptography Standards)

A series of cryptographic standards issued by the RSA Security firm in the 1990s. Of the 15 PKCS standards, the best known are probably the following:

- PKCS#1, also RFC 8017, is about RSA-based encryption and signature. An earlier version (1.5) defined an RSA encryption scheme vulnerable to Bleichenbacher's padding oracle attack. Later versions, starting with 2.0, defined instead OAEP-based RSA encryption, which is less vulnerable to padding oracle attacks.

- PKCS#7, also RFC 2315, is best known for its definition of the block cipher padding scheme but is mainly about data formatting and encoding.

- PKCS#11 is a standard API to interact with a cryptographic module, such as that of an HSM.

Poly1305

A one-time MAC best known as the authenticator component in the *ChaChaPoly* authenticated cipher, as well as ChaCha20-Poly1305. It's supported in TLS, OpenSSH, and many other applications.

FROM POLY1305 TO CHACHA20-POLY1305

In this context, *poly* refers to polynomial evaluation. To compute the MAC of a message, Poly1305 evaluates a polynomial

$$poly = c_1 r + c_2 r^2 + \cdots + c_n r^n \bmod p$$

where the c_i coefficients are blocks of the message to be authenticated and r is a 16-byte secret key. The value poly is therefore a number less than $p = 2^{130} - 5$, or $(1 \ll 130) - 5$ in pseudocode (don't write this in a C program; it won't work). The final value of the MAC is $(poly + s) \bmod 2^{128}$, where s is another 16-byte secret key.

In its initial form, Poly1305 took as input a 32-byte key k and a per-message nonce n. It then computed s by AES-encrypting n with the first 16 bytes of k as a key and using the last 16 bytes of k as r. *ChaChaPoly* computes r and s by instead hashing the key and nonce supplied to the authenticated cipher to a 32-byte string. AES is thus not used.

On paper, Poly1305 is simple, but its nonstandard arithmetic modulo $2^{130} - 5$ and key generation mechanism have sometimes proved confusing to implementers.

Polynomial complexity

Practical complexity, most of the time.

Post-compromise security

A term used mostly in the context of secure messaging to denote a notion similar to backward secrecy.

🔒 See *Backward secrecy.*

Post-quantum cryptography

Cryptography schemes designed to remain unbreakable by quantum algorithms. Therefore, they can resist the hypothetical quantum computers of the future. Also termed quantum-safe and quantum-resilient.

Post-quantum cryptography mainly targets public-key schemes (signature, encryption, key agreement) rather than symmetric schemes, because the latter are mostly immune to quantum attacks. For example, symmetric ciphers can thwart the asymptotically quadratic speedup of Grover's algorithm by simply doubling the key length, and superpolynomial speedups only occur in peculiar circumstances.

To be post-quantum, an algorithm mustn't rely on the factoring or discrete logarithm problems, both of which break when subjected to Shor's quantum algorithm. Instead, they can rely on NP-hard problems. Most of the proposed post-quantum algorithms fall into one of the following categories, depending on the hard computational problems on which they build their security:

- Code-based, relying on error-correcting codes' decoding problems

- Multivariate systems of equations

- Lattice-based, with problems such as learning with errors (LWE)

- Hash-based, or hash tree constructions using cryptographic hash functions

- Isogenies of elliptic curves

Post-quantum RSA

RSA so big that it's practically immune to quantum attacks as well as to any practical application. A public key of post-quantum RSA is of the order of one terabyte. Post-quantum RSA has been submitted to NIST's post-quantum cryptography standardization project.

Prediction resistance

A term notably used by NIST to refer to a notion similar to backward secrecy. Prediction resistance is the opposite of backtracking resistance.

🔒 See *Backward secrecy.*

Preimage

The hash function problem of finding some M so that $Hash(M) = H$ given the value H. If H was chosen by picking some M_0 at random (among a large enough finite set of possible messages) and computing $H = Hash(M_0)$, then even with unlimited computational power, an attacker can never identify M_0 with certainty unless M_0 is the only value that hashes to H.

But in practice, the message sets we deal with are much larger than the hash size; thus, any H will have many preimages. Also, nobody actually has unlimited computational power. Finding any preimage would cost 2^n, which is practically impossible, even if the hash values are as short as $n = 128$ bits.

PRESENT

Anagram of Serpent. A block cipher that works a lot like Serpent (surprise) but smaller. Marketed as an *ultra lightweight cipher*, PRESENT has 64-bit blocks like DES and supports 80-bit and 128-bit keys. According to some very academic understanding of *broken*, PRESENT is broken by biclique cryptanalysis, with respectively $2^{79.76}$ and $2^{127.91}$ complexities. But PRESENT remains safe to use, and it was standardized by ISO. A variant of PRESENT, named *GIFT*, is described as *a small PRESENT*.

PRIMES

The decisional problem of determining whether a given integer is a prime number.

PRIMES IS IN P

Known to be in the P complexity class since the 2002 AKS test, the PRIMES problem is also in NP, the class of problems for which a valid solution can be verified to be correct in polynomial time. The result that PRIMES is in NP is actually less obvious than it might sound, because it requires the demonstration of the existence of proofs of primality whose size is a polynomial function of the prime's length.

Computer scientist Vaughan Pratt first demonstrated this result in 1975, at MIT. He later commented the following in an email:

> That the primes are in NP (and hence in delta-P, the intersection of NP and co-NP) was known informally since the 1960s (i.e., well before the concept of NP itself) to the very small set of people (which Rich Schroeppel and Bob Floyd told me they belong to) who'd noticed that the Lucas–Lehmer test was not just a heuristic like many other tests for primality (which was how the LL test was invariably described back then) but actually was applicable in some sense to *every* prime. In the absence of the concept of NP, the obstacle to finding a suitable sense of this fact was the difficulty of finding

a suitable primitive root and factorizing n-1. The NP concept creates a meaningful setting in which it makes sense to simply guess a good primitive root and the factors of n-1 and then verify the guess afterwards. I'd been aware of this test since the 60s, but it was not until Karp's NP concept had appeared that I noticed that the test put the primes in NP by being applicable to every prime. I didn't think to write this up however, or even bother to mention it to anyone, since it seemed so obvious, until I mentioned it in some other context to Albert Meyer. When he said that this couldn't be true or he'd have heard about it, I wrote it up to show him, and the writeup ended up a couple of years later in print (SiComp 4:3, 214-220, 1975). The point of the every in every prime has a succinct certificate was to emphasize that the Lucas-Lehmer test was more than just a heuristic that worked only for some primes. Some minor additional analysis turned out to be necessary to make the argument stick.

A year after Pratt's publication, Gary Miller proved that PRIMES is in P if the Extended Riemann Hypothesis holds. (The hypothesis is believed to be true but remains unproven.) In 1977, Robert Solovay and Volker Strassen showed a randomized primality testing algorithm to demonstrate that PRIMES is in BPP (the class of algorithms solvable in polynomial time by randomized algorithms).

But the most common primality testing algorithm is the Miller–Rabin algorithm, a modification of Miller's initial algorithm by Michael Rabin. It's the algorithm used in most libraries when performing key generation for public-key schemes, such as RSA, that rely on prime numbers. If you run the Miller–Rabin multiple times, you can make its probability of error arbitrarily small, because it will declare a composite number as composite with probability at least $1 - (1/4)^n$ when repeated n times. Too few iterations risk mistaking composite numbers for primes. An attacker could even craft composite numbers that have an unusually high chance of being declared primes by the Miller–Rabin test, as observed in the 2018 paper "Prime and Prejudice: Primality Testing Under Adversarial Conditions."

Privacy-preserving

A broad qualifier encompassing techniques and technologies that attempt to minimize the exposure of privacy-sensitive data, such as personally identifiable information, geolocation, social graph, online activity, and so on.

The following are examples of privacy-preserving technologies, not all of which make heavy use of cryptography:

- Data analytics that processes data in a sanitized form to restrict the amount of information to what the application needs (for example, translating a person's exact age into an age range).

- Differential privacy techniques, for example, where data is made slightly inaccurate on purpose to hide its exact value, yet provides enough information to be useful.

- The Signal application's private contact discovery technique, leveraging the Intel SGX technology to prevent users' contact lists to be directly exposed to the Signal servers, yet allowing users to find out who of their contacts are using the application.

- Homomorphic encryption and searchable encryption, which can perform operations on encrypted data, thus keeping it confidential.

- Tor's onion routing, which prevents any host from knowing the source and destination of a message.

- Contact tracing protocols considered to identify COVID-19–infected persons while preventing the tracking of users' activity, social graph, and geolocation.

Private information retrieval (PIR)

Similar to oblivious transfer except the amount of information to be retrieved isn't limited. Both PIR and oblivious transfer attempt to conceal the client's activity to the database host, but PIR assumes *self-service*, whereas oblivious transfer restricts the client's access to one-in-many access.

🔒 See *Oblivious transfer.*

PROOFS OF . . .

The validation of blockchain transactions requires spending or owning some resource. This prevents arbitrary and efficient forking into alternative histories, which would enable double spending and other attacks.

This design choice has led to a renewed interest in proofs of work, which we can trace back to at least anti-spam defense in the early 1990s and to the creation of other proofs where work is something other than just CPU usage. These proofs of resource often appear motivated by blockchain applications but usually aren't specific to blockchain use cases (unlike the proof of burn).

For an inventory of some of the proposed methods—besides the main and most general notions of proof of work and proof of stake—see *Proof of burn, Proof of catalytic space, Proof of human work, Proof of reserve, Proof of sequential work, Proof of space, Proof of spacetime, Proof of storage, Proof of useful work.*

Proof of burn

Perhaps the most straightforward type of resource usage proof proposed for a consensus protocol. Proof of burn consists of nullifying the value of tokens or other digital assets associated with the protocol, for example, by sending them to some unspendable address, the blockchain equivalent of /dev/null. This differs from proofs of stake, where the value owned isn't destroyed.

Proof of catalytic space

A variant of proofs of space wherein the space isn't completely wasted but can be used to store data unrelated to the proof. This leverages the concept of catalytic space computation, where a program can use some memory region even if it's already used to store data, and return said region in its original state after completing its task.

Proof of human work

Proof of work whose work isn't a computationally intensive task but one that is relatively easy for humans, yet hard for computers and AI programs. An idea proposed it to rely on CAPTCHAs generated using obfuscated programs to prevent the machine generating CAPTCHAs to solve them.

Proof of replication

An extension of proof of storage to prove that multiple replicas of a piece of data are being stored instead of a single real copy and pointers to it. One technique used to realize proof of replication involves depth-robust graphs, a notion from graph theory rediscovered in the context of memory-hard password hashing.

Proof of reserve

Not a proof of resource associated to consensus protocols, but a proof that one account or organization owns a certain amount of coins. A proof of reserve can be publicly verifiable, for example, by issuing a special transaction from an address that controls the funds to be verified. It can also be private and/or notarized on a private ledger, for example, by signing a timestamped message provided by auditors.

A proof of reserve can be considered a proof of stake without the lottery mechanism and without being tied to any decentralized protocol.

Proof of security

🔒 See *Security proof.*

Proof of sequential work

Proof of work for which parallelism is useless, because operations must be carried out sequentially. As with parallelizable proofs of work, a solution to the puzzle must be verifiable efficiently.

Like verifiable delay functions (VDFs), proofs of sequential work can be used to add an incompressible delay in decentralized applications. They also face the same technical challenges of associating an actual time latency to a series of operations. Unlike with VDFs, a proof of sequential work doesn't admit a unique precomputable solution, which restricts its number of applications.

🔒 See *Time-lock puzzle, Verifiable delay function (VDF).*

Proof of space

A demonstration that a prover has certain amount of memory at their disposal. For example, a prover might have to allocate one terabyte to convince a verifier, and the verifier won't accept any proof from a prover that allocated less than a terabyte. Wasting memory with proofs of space is arguably more ecological than wasting CPU time with proofs of work.

Proof of spacetime

An extension of proof of storage to efficiently demonstrate that a piece of data (or multiple replicas thereof) has been stored throughout a given period of time. Proofs of spacetime can be realized by combining proofs of replication. Used by the Filecoin project, proofs of spacetime ensure that hosts rewarded to store data aren't cheating.

Proof of stake

An environment-friendly counterpart of proofs of work where miners holding a greater amount of tokens have a greater chance to validate transactions; they receive the reward by a kind of lottery system. The richest thus get richer faster by doing nothing other than *staking*, by running a node and keeping it online.

Proof of stake blockchains usually require a certain table stake amount to participate on the network.

Proof of storage

Proof that some piece of data is being stored (or at least known, or possible to be generated). Concepts such as provable data possession and proof of retrieveability are examples of proofs of storage. The most straightforward proof system is one where the verifier sends some challenge c and the prover returns $Hash(c\|M)$ where M is the data whose storage is to be verified.

Proof of useful work

When the proof of work is not completely wasteful, but compute time is used to contribute to solving some computational problem.

Proof of work

Cryptography's contribution to environmental problems.

Provable security

For some cryptographers, the only acceptable security—as opposed to unscientific, unacceptably risky heuristic security.

This simplistic goal is now less common, and provable security is now considered more of an additional insurance than as something required by all means necessary.

For example, an algorithm such as AES is not *provably secure*, and public-key schemes, such as RSA or ECDSA, are only proven secure insofar as their underlying computational problems are hard.

Provably secure

"If it's provably secure, it's probably not," to quote cryptographer Lars Knudsen (then in the context of block ciphers). This folklore adage might come from the block cipher COCONUT98, which was proven to be secure against a class of differential cryptanalysis techniques but ended up being broken by a yet unknown type of differential attack (boomerang).

Proxy re-encryption

A public-key encryption scheme where a ciphertext for Alice (created using her public key) can be turned into a ciphertext for Bob without exposing the plaintext—in other words, without decrypting and re-encrypting. For example, proxy re-encryption can be realized (in theory) thanks to indistinguishability obfuscation by creating an obfuscated program that decrypts and re-encrypts a ciphertext without exposing the plaintext.

Pseudo-random

Hyphenated spelling of *pseudorandom*. But in English, compounds created by the addition of a prefix are usually not hyphenated (for example, pseudoscience, cryptocommunist, and antisocial). Among research papers on the IACR ePrint archive, the use of *pseudorandom* is about twice as frequent as *pseudo-random*.

Pseudorandom function (PRF)

Not actually a single function but a family of many functions; each is indexed by its secret key. The security goal of a PRF is to be indistinguishable from a truly random function if you don't know the key and only see input–output pairs, even when choosing input values.

You can use PRFs as secure MACs, but a secure MAC isn't necessarily a secure PRF.

Pseudorandom number generator (PRNG)

A system generating random-looking data with the security guarantee that an attacker that knows any subset of the output bits cannot determine any other output bits. The theoretical definition of a PRNG differs from its colloquial usage.

In theory, a PRNG is a (deterministic) algorithm that takes as input a value (seed) of fixed size and returns a longer output value. In practice, a PRNG often refers to all the components involved in the generation of pseudorandom bits, for example, in the context of an operating system's PRNG. Such a PRNG usually includes the following components:

- Entropy collectors from analog sources, such as user activity, temperature measurements, and on-chip sensors—sometimes referred to as true random generators, although their (digital) output is rarely guaranteed to be cryptographically safe, or even uniformly distributed.

- A mechanism to store an internal state, such as *entropy pools*, including the logic to update it and perform *reseeding* operations from entropy collectors.

- A deterministic random bit generator (DRBG), which produces an arbitrarily long output from a seed derived from the internal state.

Pseudorandom permutation (PRP)

To a permutation what a PRF is to a hash function. A block cipher is a PRP.

Public-key cryptography

All cryptography, excluding symmetric cryptography.

PUF (physically unclonable function)

A physical component on semiconductor devices that leverages minute differences between each different platform to generate unpredictable values, such as identifiers. Although sometimes advertised as semi-magical technology, many PUFs have been shown to be cryptographically weaker than claimed.

Puncturable encryption

Public-key encryption augmented with a *puncture* operation. This operation creates a new private key to replace the current one to forever revoke the decryption capability for certain ciphertexts that the previous key could decrypt. One motivation for this is to be able to provide forward secrecy for certain messages, even though they were encrypted with the same public key.

You can create puncturable symmetric encryption from puncturable PRFs.

Puncturable pseudorandom function (PPRF)

Similar to puncturable encryption. PRFs whose keys can be updated to revoke the capability to process certain values.

Quantum computer

According to some experts, has a 1/7 chance of breaking RSA-2048 by 2026 and a 1/2 chance by 2031. In truth, nobody knows if you'll see a quantum computer breaking RSA-2048 in your lifetime.

Quantum cryptography

Cryptographic operations that rely on quantum phenomena and don't necessarily need a quantum computer, such as quantum key distribution. Quantum cryptography happens to be post-quantum but doesn't belong to the field of post-quantum cryptography.

Quantum encryption

Encryption of quantum states as opposed to strings of classical bits. The most basic form of this is the quantum one-time pad, which you can think of as a combination of quantum teleportation (to transmit the encrypted state) and a classical one-time pad (the bits required to read the decrypted state).

The quantum one-time pad looks less efficient than its classical counterpart, requiring two classical bits of key for each bit of information encrypted. But it's also more powerful, because it can be leveraged to build secure homomorphic and multi-party computation schemes.

Quantum key distribution

Sometimes confused with post-quantum cryptography, but different and of lower practical value. The best known is the *BB84* key agreement protocol

🔓 See *BB84*.

Quantum signature

An impossible scheme, because the classical notion of a signature doesn't apply to quantum states. Intuitively, you should see why: any party that can learn information about a quantum state can also modify it. In particular, it's impossible to attach a signature to a quantum state, as you would do with a classical message. More generally, quantum states cannot be authenticated unless they're also encrypted, so that only the intended recipient can decrypt them. But although quantum signing isn't possible, quantum signcryption is.

QUIC (Quick UDP Internet Connections)

A transport security protocol designed to make HTTPS connections more reliable under poor conditions (packet loss, IP roaming, and so on), notably by running over UDP rather than TCP. Using UDP saves it from the latency cost of the TCP handshake. It also includes some mechanism to mitigate the problem of UDP's unreliability. HTTP-over-QUIC has been officially standardized by IETF and has been named HTTP/3.

Rabin cryptosystem

RSA with 2 as a public exponent, kinda. Because computing modular square roots is proven to be equivalent to factoring, breaking Rabin encryption is as hard as factoring its modulus $n = pq$. The equivalence between breaking RSA and factoring is harder to demonstrate.

Rainbow tables

Time-memory trade-off technique mostly applied to password cracking, such as Windows NTLM passwords. Rainbow tables are a specific, optimized type of look-up tables precomputed once, in the *offline* stage, to significantly speed up the cracking of passwords (*online* stage).

Rainbow tables are also successfully applied to crack pay-TV control words within short cryptoperiods (such as 10 seconds). They're designed and often also made in Switzerland.

Random bits

Bits that have been generated at random. We often talk of random bits when strictly speaking they've only been pseudorandomly generated.

Random oracle

An abstract concept used to prove that a protocol is secure in theory: you can imagine a random oracle as a function $f()$ that, every time you send it an input x, it picks a random value y and returns it as the output while registering $f(x) = y$. This sounds similar to how a hash function ought to behave, yet a random oracle relies on a slightly different assumption than that of a secure hash function. Assuming that a hash function is a random oracle makes it easier to write security proofs. But such proofs are perceived as less reliable because, unlike secure hash functions, random oracles can't exist in practice, but in practice that's not a concern.

Randomness

The most important thing in cryptography. Without randomness, you couldn't generate random secret values so there would be no secret keys and therefore no encryption. Even if you already have keys, you need randomness to achieve the highest public-key encryption security level (called *semantic security, or IND-CPA*).

Range proof

Proof that a number lies in a certain interval without having to reveal the number (the zero-knowledge part). Some cryptocurrencies use range proofs to hide the amounts transferred, and to ensure the correctness of a protocol's execution, for example.

RC4

Rivest's Cipher 4, designed in 1987. A stream cipher with a tumultuous history: initially, it was a proprietary algorithm from the firm RSA Security and was then reverse engineered and published in 1994. It withstood cryptanalysis surprisingly well despite its extreme simplicity and lack of academic peer-review seal of approval—until it didn't, and was found to be insecure (because of statistical biases in the first bytes it generates). Still, it was less insecure than most proprietary algorithms from that era. RC4 was the basis of WEP, the first Wi-Fi encryption scheme, which was broken in part because of RC4's properties but in larger part because of WEP's flawed design. RC4 was also used in TLS, where its statistical biases could be exploited to decrypt data that is encrypted under many different keys. Because of its small size, RC4 is also used in malware to obfuscate code or encrypt data sent to the malware's server.

RC5

A cipher whose only commonality with RC4 is its designer Ronald Rivest; unlike RC4, RC5 is not a stream cipher but a block cipher. RC5 is one of the few ciphers to use data-dependent rotations, an idea that at first sounds like it makes the cipher more complicated. But it also turned out to facilitate cryptanalysis, because an attacker could then control the rotation values.

RC6

Similar to RC5. Also a block cipher that uses data-dependent rotations and was patented by RSA Security. Designed by Ronald Rivest (along with other people) as well, RC6 was one of the candidates in the AES competition. It wasn't chosen by NIST to be the AES but was later used in a software implant allegedly designed by the NSA.

Real world

Academic cryptography's term to refer to reality, as opposed to the *ideal world* of the security models needed to rigorously analyze the security of cryptographic schemes. If attackers in the real world are less powerful than in the ideal world, then security proofs on paper guarantee real security.

The term is often the source of pleonasms, for example: *previous works don't clarify how the code should be instantiated concretely in the real world, real-world applications*, and *practical real-world protocols*.

Real World Crypto (RWC)

A cryptography conference focused on current real applications of cryptography, as opposed to research conferences less concerned with direct applications. Attended by participants from academia and industry, it's the largest cryptography conference in terms of participants. RWC is held alternately on the US West Coast, East Coast, in Europe, and in the Asia-Pacific region. Speakers present contributed talks (which aren't necessarily from formal research papers) with titles such as "Privacy-Preserving Telemetry in Firefox" and "Weaknesses in the Moscow Internet Voting System."

🔒 See *Asiacrypt, CHES, CRYPTO, Eurocrypt, FSE, PKC, TCC*.

Rectangle attack

An improvement of the boomerang attack, created to attack the block cipher Serpent.

🔒 See *Boomerang attack*.

Related-key attack

An attack that makes encryption or decryption queries for instances of the cipher whose key is a modified version of the original key, so the modification (as a function) is chosen by the attacker. For example, a related-key attack on a block cipher might make encryption queries $\text{Enc}(K \oplus M, P)$ where M is a fixed value defined by the attacker without knowing the key.

You can only use this attack model against symmetric primitives, because it would be too powerful and effective against public-key schemes. Related-key attacks aren't a very realistic threat when the key is secret.

Research papers

What academic researchers must write to keep their jobs. The IACR's ePrint server received 69 research papers in 2000, 661 in 2010, and 1,499 in 2019. No one has time to read all these articles, which is why it's crucial for researchers to write succinct, informative abstracts, as well as clear and appealing titles.

FUN WITH PAPER TITLES

Conventional paper titles are boring; they usually follow the structure "New X for Solving Problem Y Using Technique Z." But researchers sometimes get creative with titles, such as the following:

"Proof of Work Proves Not to Work"

"Dumb Crypto in Smart Grids"

"FourQ: Four-Dimensional Decompositions on a Q-curve over the Mersenne Prime"

"Mining Your Ps and Qs: Detection of Widespread Weak Keys in Network Devices"

"Prime and Prejudice: Primality Testing Under Adversarial Conditions"

"The Hunting of the SNARK"

Revocation

Problem solved in theory but rarely in practice.

Rijndael

The block cipher that became known as AES after winning the AES competition in 2000. The Rijndael name is a portmanteau of the last names of its designers, Belgian cryptographers Joan Daemen and Vincent Rijmen. The Google query *how do you say rijndael* returns about 100,000 results.

🔒 See *AES*.

Ring signature

First described in the paper "How to Leak a Secret" by Rivest, Shamir, and Tauman. Ring signatures involve a group of signers such that any signer can create a signature that is signer-ambiguous with respect to the subset of signers of their choice. In other words, verifiers have no way of identifying the signer; they can only know the group of potential signers that they're in. Unlike with group signatures, there is no way to deanonymize the signer.

🔒 See *Group signature*.

RIPEMD-160

A hash function designed in 1992. RIPEMD-160 got a second life due to its use in Bitcoin and many other cryptocurrencies.

Rivest-Shamir-Adleman

The authors of the 1978 paper "A Method for Obtaining Digital Signatures and Public-Key Cryptosystems" that described the RSA cryptosystem. RSA's then unique property was that the key used for encryption is different from the one used for decryption. RSA has evolved into standardized schemes to encrypt and sign securely (such as the OAEP and PSS standards, respectively). But its market share has declined while elliptic-curve cryptography has gained greater adoption. But RSA's support for *native*, non-hybrid encryption, as well as fast signature verification, sometimes makes it the best option when these properties are necessary.

Ronald Rivest, Adi Shamir, and Leonard Adleman noted the following direct consequences of their new cryptosystem in their 1978 paper:

1. Couriers or other secure means are not needed to transmit keys, since a message can be enciphered using an encryption key publicly revealed by the intended recipient. Only he can decipher the message, since only he knows the corresponding decryption key.

2. A message can be *signed* using a privately held decryption key. Anyone can verify this signature using the corresponding publicly revealed encryption key. Signatures cannot be forged, and a signer cannot later deny the validity of his signature. This has obvious applications in *electronic mail* and *electronic funds transfer* systems.

ROBOT (Return Of Bleichenbacher's Oracle Threat)

Bleichenbacher's attack, 20 years later.

🔒 See *Bleichenbacher attack*.

ROS

Random inhomogeneities in an Overdetermined Solvable system of linear equations: the hardest of all crypto abbreviations to memorize.

RSA

The biggest conference in the information security industry.

Rubber-hose cryptanalysis

Term popularized by XKCD's comic 538. A reminder that mathematical cryptographic adversarial models often fail to capture more mundane risks from procedural or human flaws.

Rumba20

The only hash function from the Salsa20 family. Rumba20 was created in the context of new results regarding the generalized birthday problem.

SAEP (Simplified OAEP)

A variant of OAEP that is slightly simpler and achieves the same level of chosen-ciphertext security.

🔓 See *OAEP (Optimal Asymmetric Encryption Padding)*.

Salsa20

Undoubtedly one of the most influential cryptographic algorithms. It led to the stream cipher ChaCha20 (used in TLS, SSH, and many other places). This in turn was reused in the BLAKE2 hash function, a component of the Argon2 password hash and protocols such as WireGuard. More generally, Salsa20 popularized simple, easy to implement add-rotate-xor (ARX) constructions. A few years earlier, NIST had standardized a more complicated cipher whose understanding required the knowledge of concepts such as polynomials, matrix inversion, and finite fields.

The 20 in Salsa20 is for its number of rounds, a conservative value initially chosen by its designer and later relaxed in some applications, decreasing to 12 or even 8.

Sandwich attack

A refinement of the boomerang attack often used to cryptanalyze block ciphers. A sandwich attack relies on a distinguisher divided into three parts: "A thick slice (bread) at the top, a thin slice (meat) in the middle, and a thick slice (bread) at the bottom." It was invented to find the first practical attack on the block cipher KASUMI.

🔓 See *Boomerang attack*.

S-box

A look-up table used in block ciphers to implement a nonlinear transformation with measurable security properties (such as nonlinearity or branch number), although S-boxes are not necessarily implemented as look-up tables. In the context of differential cryptanalysis, an active S-box is one for which the values from the two (different) inputs yield a different input value to the S-box, and thus a different output.

S-boxes are usually 4-bit (16 values, as in Serpent) or 8-bit (256 values, as in Rijndael/AES).

Scalar

A number, as opposed to a vector or group element, for example. When you hear *scalar multiplication* in cryptography, it often just means multiplication of a point on an elliptic curve by a number, according to the addition law defined on said curve.

sci.crypt

Along with sci.crypt.research, Usenet newsgroup where people discussed cryptography before Twitter and Slack. It's notorious for its can-you-break-my-cipher-here's-a-ciphertext posts.

Scrambler

Former term for ciphers used in telecommunications and audio/video content processing. The first of these algorithms were cryptographically weak, because they didn't really encrypt the signal but effectively just made it unintelligible. The later algorithms evolved into actual cryptography.

🔒 See *DVB-CSA*.

scrypt

A password hash function with configurable time memory usage, pronounced *ess-crypt*. scrypt pioneered memory-hard password hashing and inspired subsequent designs as well as the Password Hashing Competition.

scrypt has a modular, if not outright minimalistic, design. It includes, as subcomponents, the PBKDF2 construction based on HMAC-SHA-256 as well as the Salsa20/8 stream cipher.

Searchable encryption

Encryption of database records that allows a search on encrypted data. For example, it permits a search that given an encrypted keyword retrieves the encrypted items that, when decrypted, include the keyword.

Searchable encryption schemes that are possibly practical and useful leak some information about the encrypted data. In contrast, those with the highest security guarantees are severely limited functionality- and performance-wise (for example, those using functional encryption, homomorphic encryption, and oblivious RAMs).

secp256k1

The elliptic curve used by Bitcoin, Ethereum, and many other crypto- currencies for their ECDSA signatures of transactions. The k indicates a Koblitz curve. Unlike other standard curves, and in particular unlike the ubiquitous secp256r1 (also known as the NIST p-256), secp256k1 doesn't rely on pseudorandom parameters and is in principle less likely to have been manipulated. The actual reasons why Satoshi Nakamoto, or whoever, chose to use secp256k1 remain unclear.

Secret sharing

🔒 See *Threshold secret sharing.*

Security

An important aspect of cryptographic schemes. Security of a cryp- tographic scheme on paper doesn't imply security in reality (to some extent, the reverse is also true). Even the existence of a formal proof that a cryptographic scheme is secure doesn't necessarily mean it's secure in all real-life conditions, because the definition of "secure in practice" is often undefinable in mathematical terms.

Security proof

The demonstration that finding an algorithm to break some new crypto scheme is at least as hard as finding an algorithm to break some other crypto scheme or notoriously hard math problem, or a reduction of one problem to another. Security proofs only prove an algorithm's security insofar as their assumptions about attackers' capabilities are accurate. Also, the scheme on which it's based must really be practically unbreak- able. Other caveats include the fact that the reduction might be too loose to be meaningful, and that, in reality, breaking cryptography isn't always about attacking an algorithm.

Semantic security

🔒 See *IND-CPA.*

Serious Cryptography

Yet another book about cryptography.

Serpent

In hindsight, would have been a good choice as the AES standard: its design is easy to understand, because it contains no finite fields, polynomials, matrix multiplication, or other such math; its implementation logic doesn't stray too far from the specification; and it poses no risk of cache-timing attacks. But its security margin (in other words, number of rounds) involved perhaps too much crypto compared to Rijndael.

🔒 See *PRESENT*.

SHA-0

First draft of SHA-1.

SHA-1

A secure hash function if the only security you need is preimage resistance. It took approximately 12 years to progress from the collision attack described in a 2005 paper to a demonstrable collision in 2017.

SHA-2

Not one but four hash functions:

- SHA-256 looks like SHA-1 but with more rounds and more complex internals.
- SHA-224 is SHA-256 with 224-bit output instead of 256-bit output.
- SHA-512 looks like SHA-256 with 64-bit words instead of 32-bit words.
- SHA-384 is SHA-512 with 384-bit output instead of 512-bit output.

Unlike SHA-1, SHA-2 algorithms aren't broken and are unlikely to ever be.

SHA-3

When someone tells you they use SHA-3, you should ask which version of SHA-3 they use: it could be SHA3-224, SHA3-256, SHA3-384, SHA3-512, SHAKE128, or SHAKE256. If it's one of the latter two, you might want to know what output length they use, because these aren't simple hash functions but XOF (extendable-output functions).

🔒 See *Keccak*.

SHA-3 competition

Officially the *NIST hash function competition*. The 2008 to 2012 selection process for SHA-3 eventually settled on Keccak after a final round that included BLAKE, Grøstl, JH, and Skein. Of 64 submissions received by NIST, 51 were accepted as valid.

SHA-3 PANDEMONIUM

The first few months of the SHA-3 competition were a rampage. Most submissions by amateurs were broken, sometimes within minutes of reading their specification.

Noteworthy submissions included:

- MD6: Tree-based hash having nothing to do with MD5 but its designer
- CubeHash: Minimalist ChaCha-like permutation-based
- ECOH, FSB, SWIFFTX: Attempts of provably secure hashes using a reduction to a hard computational problem

SHACAL

A block cipher extracted from the compression function used in SHA-1. More precisely, SHACAL is the keyed permutation in SHA-1's instance of a Davies–Meyer construction. Likewise, SHACAL-2 is SHA-256's block cipher; it was submitted to the NESSIE project and was selected.

SHACAL is pronounced like the French *chacal*, meaning jackal.

Shamir's secret database

A list of all prime numbers—and therefore all RSA private keys—that Adi Shamir is rumored to have created to instantaneously break RSA. To the best of our knowledge, this rumor has never been confirmed or denied.

Shor's algorithm

A quantum algorithm that solves factoring and discrete logarithms with practical complexity. Shor's algorithm is the reason the field of post-quantum cryptography exists.

SHS (Secure Hash Standard)

The FIPS 180-4 document that specifies the SHA-1 and SHA-2 algorithms, "for computing a condensed representation of electronic data (message)."

SHA-3 is specified in a separate document titled "SHA-3 Standard: Permutation-Based Hash and Extendable-Output Functions" (FIPS 202).

Side channel

Any way to obtain information about a cryptographic operation other than the specified output values.

Side-channel attack

An attack that leverages some side-channel information, either passively or actively, locally or remotely, based on physical or logical properties. A side-channel attack doesn't necessarily require physical access to the module attacked.

KINDS OF SIDE CHANNELS

Here is an incomplete list of classes of side-channel attacks:

- Timing attacks when the execution time depends on sensitive data
- Fault attacks, such as CPU overclocking, power glitching, and laser fault injection
- Simple measurement of differential analysis of physical phenomena: acoustic waves, electromagnetic emanations, and heat
- Operating system leaks, via procfs, dmesg entries, race conditions, and various ASLR leaks
- Traffic analysis over encrypted communications
- Micro-architectural attacks, such as cache attacks
- Shoulder surfing and observation of users' movements

Sigaba

The American Enigma, designed in the 1930s. It was never officially broken.

Signal protocol

The combination of the X3DH session initialization protocol and the double ratchet state update and key update protocol, as used by the Signal application. A similar protocol was integrated in WhatsApp and Facebook Messenger, reusing libraries developed for Signal. The cryptographic research and engineering behind the Signal protocol had a major impact on secure messaging applications.

🔓 See *Double ratchet, X3DH*.

Signature

Public-key signature, or digital signature, but different from electronic signature, e-signature, or electromagnetic signature. It's sometimes sacrilegiously defined as *encrypting with the private key*.

WHAT IS THE SECURITY GOAL OF A SIGNATURE?

A brilliant CS master's student once successfully defended his master's thesis project (on post-quantum cryptography). In the Q&A part of his defense, after questions about his work, his cryptography professor asked him, "What's the security goal of a signature?"

The student was confused by this deceptively simple question.

Signatures should be unforgeable under adaptive chosen-message attacks. An attacker who can query a valid signer for a signature of any message of their choice shouldn't be able to compute a signature for any other message.

The student thus unconvincingly answered, "Existential unforgeability under adaptive chosen-message attacks."

The professor said that no, this wasn't the unique goal of public-key signatures because, after all, MACs attempt to achieve a similar goal.

The professor had expected the answer *nonrepudiation*, or the property that a signer cannot claim that someone else issued the signature on their behalf, because nobody else knows the private signing key. The same isn't true for MACs. This notion is intuitively the opposite of deniability, although in MACs can effectively provide nonrepudiation if a signature was demonstrably transmitted by some entity or computer.

A more flexible form of nonrepudiation is provided by undeniable signatures, which are defined in this book, along with many other signature variants (blind, group, ring, threshold, and so on).

Signcryption

To public-key cryptography what authenticated encryption is to symmetric cryptography. In other words, signcryption is signature and encryption within a single primitive.

SIKE (Supersingular Isogeny Key Encapsulation)

Sounds like BIKE. SIKE is also a post-quantum KEM but is based on an isogeny problem rather than a decoding problem.

SIKE is based on SIDH (Supersingular Isogeny Diffie–Hellman), the main isogeny-based key agreement scheme, and is a candidate in NIST's post-quantum project.

🔒 See *BIKE (Bit Flipping Key Encapsulation), Isogeny-based cryptography.*

SIMECK

SIMON + SPECK = SIMECK. It's a block cipher that borrows from the SIMON and SPECK NSA-designed ciphers to create an algorithm suitable for software- and hardware-constrained implementations. SIMECK is not from the NSA.

SIMON

Along with its brother SPECK, block ciphers designed to qualify as lightweight, optimized for hardware and software, respectively. SIMON would likely be used in many projects if it wasn't designed by the NSA. Indeed, arguing that Caesar's wife must be above suspicion, many cryptographers objected to the use of SIMON and SPECK after Snowden publicly questioned the NSA's trustworthiness.

SipHash

Not a hash but a pseudorandom function. SipHash is used as a secure MAC and is optimized for short input values. It was designed to prevent hash-flooding attacks against hash tables.

SIV-AES

AES in SIV mode. For some reason, it's not called AES-SIV. Instead, it goes by the official name of *Synthetic Initialization Vector (SIV) Authenticated Encryption Using the Advanced Encryption Standard (AES)*. Not to be confused with AES-GCM-SIV.

As with AES-GCM-SIV, SIV-AES avoids the hazard of exposing plaintext data if the same nonce is used more than once. SIV-AES also uses the trick of deriving the encryption nonce from the message, thus leading to different nonces for different messages.

Unlike AES-GCM-SIV, the MAC used in SIV-AES isn't based on binary polynomial multiplication. Instead, it uses the AES-based CMAC, a variant of CBC-MAC. (Perhaps you remember AES-CCM?) This contributes to making SIV-AES simpler than AES-GCM-SIV but also slightly less fast.

Skipjack

A block cipher designed by the NSA in the late 1980s. It's famous for its role in the Clipper fiasco and is currently often used as a toy cipher in cryptanalysis classes. Skipjack hasn't been fully broken or shown to include a backdoor.

🔒 See *Clipper*.

Slide attack

An attack introduced in a 1999 paper that began as follows: "It is a general belief among the designers of block-ciphers that even a relatively weak cipher may become very strong if its number of rounds is made very large."

The paper then goes on to describe a type of attack on block ciphers that works regardless of the number of rounds used.

Slide attacks work as follows:

Assume that the encryption function $E()$ works by iterating a round function $R()$, such that $E(X) = R(R(\ldots R(X) \ldots))$. The attack first looks for one or more *slid pairs*, which are pairs of plaintext blocks X and Y such that $R(X) = Y$, and therefore $E(X) = R^{-1}(E(Y))$. You can use several tricks to identify these pairs.

Once you have such pairs, breaking the cipher is equivalent to just breaking one round, which is usually easy.

SM

A suite of Chinese national cryptographic standards, including publicly available algorithms that certain products in China are required to use. The SM suite includes elliptic-curve public-key cryptography (SM2), a hash function (SM3), a block cipher (SM4), and, interestingly, identity-based cryptography (SM9).

Smart contract

Programs running on blockchain platforms. Bugs in smart contracts tend to have catastrophic consequences.

Snake-oil

Bruce Schneier's snake-oil warning signs from 1999 are still applicable today:

1. Pseudo-mathematical gobbledygook
2. New mathematics
3. Proprietary cryptography
4. Extreme cluelessness
5. Ridiculous key lengths
6. One-time pads
7. Unsubstantiated claims
8. Security proofs
9. Cracking contests

SNARK (succinct non-interactive argument of knowledge)

A powerful and efficient type of proof of knowledge. Introduced in the 2011 article "From Extractable Collision Resistance to Succinct Non-Interactive Arguments of Knowledge, and Back Again." It's a variant of a SNARG (succinct non-interactive argument), because a SNARK is a *SNARG of knowledge*. SNARKs can, for example, be used for (noninteractive) delegation of computation, where a worker uses a SNARK to prove that they performed the correct computation.

When a SNARK is zero-knowledge, we talk of zk-SNARK, which was famously used in the Zcash blockchain protocol to anonymize transactions via a proof that tokens have been transferred from a sender to a recipient without disclosing either's identity or the amount transferred.

Post-quantum SNARKs exist but are less efficient than pre-quantum ones.

DISSECTING SNARKS

The following explains SNARK word by word, starting from the end:

An *argument of knowledge* is essentially a proof of knowledge that is practically secure, whereas *proof of knowledge* is, strictly speaking, reserved for proofs that remain secure against computationally unbounded adversaries. In the context of cryptographic applications, the *knowledge* proved can be that of a secret value or of the relation between values that must be kept secret.

Non-interactive just means that the SNARK comes as a single message from a prover to a verifier rather than as a protocol involving multiple messages.

Succinct means that the message is of a relatively small size, even if the argument covers large amounts of data, and that it's efficiently verifiable.

SNIP (secret-shared non-interactive proof)

A zero-knowledge protocol with one prover and several verifiers that each holds a share of a proof of correctness. Each verifier holds a share of the secret value; the prover sends distinct proof strings to each verifier, allowing the verifiers to collaborate to check the validity of the secret according to some predefined predicate without leaking any information on said secret. SNIPs were introduced as a tool to build privacy-preserving aggregate statistics schemes.

SNOW 3G

A stream cipher used in 3G, 4G, and 5G communications to encrypt voice communications. Like its early predecessor A5/1, SNOW 3G works by updating a state composed of feedback shift registers, which makes it simple to implement and efficient. Unlike A5/1, SNOW 3G is secure. A new version of SNOW 3G for 5G networks called *SNOW-V* was proposed in 2020 to be faster in software, because 5G relies a lot more on software and virtualized environments than previous standards.

🔒 See *Feedback shift register.*

Solitaire

A stream cipher created by Bruce Schneier for the novel *Cryptonomicon*. The novel's characters use it without accessing a computer. As Schneier describes:

> Solitaire gets its security from the inherent randomness in a shuffled deck of cards. By manipulating this deck, a communicant can create a string of *random* letters that he then combines with his message. Of course Solitaire can be simulated on a computer, but it is designed to be implemented by hand.

Solitaire is broken by today's academic standards (it has a statistical bias), but it's quite secure for a pen-and-paper cipher, and practically safe when used correctly.

🔒 See *Cryptonomicon*.

SPECK

An NSA lightweight cipher.

🔒 See *SIMON*.

SPEKE (Simple Password Exponential Key Exchange)

PAKE invented long before PAKEs were cool (in 1996).

SPHINCS

A hash-based signature scheme that, unlike XMSS, is stateless. But it's even more complicated than XMSS. Gravity-SPHINCS and SPHINCS+ are SPHINCS variants that were submitted to NIST's post-quantum competition. Not to be confused with the SPHINX mixnet.

🔒 See *XMSS*.

Sponge function

The simplest way to design a hash function. A sponge function uses only a permutation algorithm—as opposed to a keyed permutation—or a block cipher. Pioneered by Keccak, now SHA-3, it leads to a multitude of permutation-based schemes.

🔒 See *Keccak, Permutation-based cryptography*.

SRP (Secure Remote Password)

PAKE relying on the Diffie–Hellman problem. SRP can be combined with TLS and is notably used in iCloud Keychain. But overall, it's found in very few applications, most likely because of vulnerabilities in earlier versions of SRP, and because the minor security benefit is often not worth SRP's extra complexity compared to a straightforward password authentication.

SSH (Secure Shell)

A secure channel over TCP. SSH relies on neither PKI nor X.509 certificates. Instead, it has a trust-on-first-use (TOFU) trust model. Fewer security issues have been found in SSH than in TLS.

SSL (Secure Socket Layer)

Not TLS. SSL is the predecessor of that ubiquitous transport security protocol; it was designed in the 1990s by Netscape and had three versions, the first of which was never released because it was too insecure. SSL v2 shipped with Netscape Navigator 1.1 in March 1995, and SSL v3 was released shortly after to notably mitigate a man-in-the-middle attack (working by downgrading to a weak cipher suite). Nonetheless, many systems continued to support SSL v2, sometimes for backward compatibility. Twenty years later, the DROWN attack exploited such legacy support of SSL v2 to attack recent TLS versions.

🔒 See *TLS.*

STARK (scalable transparent arguments of knowledge)

Variants of SNARKs. STARKs were motivated by applications requiring efficient and scalable zero-knowledge proofs with fewer constraints than with SNARKs. Here are the main differences between STARKs and SNARKs:

- STARKs don't require a *trusted setup*—a process that must be performed by trusted parties so that subsequent proofs are secure.

- STARKs can be safe against quantum algorithms, whereas known SNARK constructions usually aren't (or with some constraints).

- STARKs are a bit faster to create and a bit slower to verify.

🔒 See *SNARK (succinct non-interactive argument of knowledge).*

Steganography

Covert communication techniques that belong more to the field of signal processing than to cryptography.

Stream cipher

A type of cipher you can think of as a one-time pad cryptographically generated from a key and a (unique) nonce. The block cipher DES was designed in the 1970s with hardware implementations in mind; later the stream cipher RC4 was designed to be software friendly due to its byte-oriented mechanism. Yet in the 1990s stream ciphers were often thought of as *hardware ciphers* and were frequently based on feedback shift registers with minimal surrounding logic, like Grain or SNOW 3G. On the other hand, block ciphers are considered software ciphers, as the AES competition requirements made clear in 2000. Indeed, you'll find stream ciphers used in niche, constrained applications, even before the term *lightweight cryptography* existed, when block ciphers were too costly.

Today, stream ciphers are no longer a niche market, and many of the encryption modes used in modern applications are technically stream ciphers because they run in CTR mode.

STREAM CIPHER MODES

Historically, stream ciphers could have two modes:

- Synchronous, also known as autonomous or key auto key (KAK). The more well-known mode whereby a pseudorandom keystream is generated and XORed to the message.

- Self-synchronizing, also known as autoclave or ciphertext auto key (CTAK), where the output depends on the message encryption.

Substitution-permutation network (SPN)

Construction of permutations, as used in block ciphers and hash functions, in which a round includes two layers:

- Substitution, typically via S-boxes, to transform chunks of blocks into other chunks in a nonlinear manner (that is, with a complex input–output relation). This strong but very local transformation is sometimes said to bring *confusion*.

- Permutation, typically via shuffling of bits or a matrix operation to make sure that each output bit will eventually depend on all input bits. This is weak, but block-wise transformation is said to provide *diffusion*.

In an SPN, these two layers are complementary, and this separation of duties often simplifies the analysis of the cipher and the calculation of bounds on the success rate of certain attack techniques. AES, Serpent, and PRESENT are examples of SPNs.

Suck

As defined by cryptographer Matthew Green: "In cryptography *suck* is a purely technical term meaning *slow, complex*, and *probably insecure*."

Sugar beet auctions

For many years, the only known real-world application of multi-party computation (MPC). Sugar beet auctions occurred in Denmark in 2008 with the support of Aarhus University researchers. They were described in detail in the paper "Secure Multiparty Computation Goes Live" and cited in numerous other papers as evidence that MPC isn't useless. Thanks to blockchain protocols, there are now many more MPC applications.

Suite A

The NSA's suite of classified cryptographic algorithms and techniques. Suite A is used, for example, in military secure communication devices. It's not available to the public.

🔒 See **NSA (National Security Agency)**.

A PEEK INTO SUITE A

Suite A seems to include a number of interesting ciphers, such as the following:

- BATON, a block cipher developed by the NSA around 1995. It has a 128-bit-long block and a key of 320 bits, 160 of which are checksum bits (which means that BATON's key only has 160 secret bits). BATON is supported by the PKCS#11 cryptography interface standard; thus BATON's parameters and supported modes are publicly documented. These modes include an undocumented *SHUFFLE* mode as well as a key wrapping mode. BATON is one of the fastest NSA ciphers.

᛭ SAVILLE, a stream cipher developed by the NSA jointly with the British GCHQ in the late 1960s. It was used notably in encryption devices during the Vietnam War. SAVILLE is based on a nonlinear feedback shift register and uses a 128-bit key whose last eight bits are a checksum of the first 120 bits. SAVILLE has the interesting property of being able to run in synchronous or self-synchronizing mode.

Suite A also includes algorithms such as ACCORDION, CRAYON, JUNIPER, and PHALANX.

SUPERCOP

System for Unified Performance Evaluation Related to Cryptographic Operations and Primitives. It's a successor of BATMAN and eBASH.

SUPERCOP estimates the optimal speed of an algorithm by trying out many different implementations of it. It also compiles each implementation with many different compiler options and then runs the compiled program multiple times to reliably measure its execution time. As of May 2020, SUPERCOP has benchmarked more than 1,000 different algorithms and more than 2,800 implementations of them, as well as multiple compilers and compiler options.

In terms of CPU usage, running SUPERCOP is to cryptography implementers what Bitcoin mining is to cryptocurrency people.

Superpolynomial complexity

Practically impossible complexity, according to Cobham's thesis (and empirical observation).

SVP (shortest vector problem)

The main computational problem in lattice-based cryptography. SVP involves finding a combination of multidimensional vectors whose length (with respect to a given norm) is the smallest.

Many lattice-based cryptosystems indirectly leverage the worst-case hardness of an SVP-like problem, such as GapSVP, due to results relating the learning with errors (LWE) problem to SVP problems.

Symmetric-key cryptography

The oldest form of post-quantum cryptography.

TCC

The Theory of Cryptography Conference "focuses on paradigms, approaches, and techniques used to conceptualize, define, and provide solutions to natural cryptographic problems."

TCC indeed covers both theoretical cryptography—an intellectually interesting topic but of low practical relevance, for example, when concerned with concepts such as quantum random oracles—and the theoretical aspects of applied cryptography, where fundamental results can be of high practical interest.

Researchers present peer-reviewed research papers with titles such as "Obfuscated Fuzzy Hamming Distance and Conjunctions from Subset Product Problems" and "Fully Homomorphic NIZK and NIWI Proofs."

🔒 See *Asiacrypt, CHES, CRYPTO, Eurocrypt, FSE, PKC, Real World Crypto.*

Test vectors

Alas, often the only tests found in cryptosystems' implementations.

Threefish

The third member of the Blowfish family but very different from Blowfish and Twofish. It has no Feistel network, no MDS matrices, no S-box, but just an ARX construction allegedly inspired by ChaCha and that later inspired SipHash.

Threshold encryption

Strictly speaking, doesn't exist. But threshold decryption does exist. It's where the decryption key is threshold-shared among N parties, $t \leq N$ of which must collaborate to decrypt a ciphertext.

Threshold secret-sharing

Or just secret sharing. A mechanism whereby a secret is split into N shares so that $t \leq N$ are required to recover the secret, and fewer than t don't reveal information about the secret. Shamir's method, based on polynomial interpolation, is the standard way to realize secret sharing.

Verifiable secret-sharing (VSS) is a variant wherein parties can cryptographically verify that the correct secret has been recovered and that each party provided their correct share.

Threshold signature

A signature scheme where signing capabilities (that is, keys) are distributed across N potential signers and where a signature requires at least $t \leq N$ signatures from distinct signers. It's notably used for custody of cryptocurrency in cold storage systems of certain exchanges.

Time AI™

The Fyre Festival of cryptography.

Time-lock encryption

A cryptographic time capsule. Time-lock encryption attempts to make decryption impossible—even with the decryption key—until a certain date, when the algorithm authorizes noninteractive decryption. Like many cryptographic functionalities, you can achieve it using a trusted execution environment under fairly realistic assumptions. It's also possible to create time-locked ciphertexts by leveraging so-called computational reference clocks, like those obtained from blockchains.

Time-lock puzzle

The first instance of *timed-release crypto*. It was defined in 1996 as a way to "send information into the future" by creating a problem whose solution is known by its creator but the recovery of which otherwise requires a large amount of computation. It later inspired time-lock encryption.

🔒 See *Proof of sequential work, Verifiable delay function (VDF)*.

THE FAILURE OF THE TIME-LOCK PUZZLE

In 1999, authors of the time-lock puzzle paper proposed an actual challenge, and they made the following prediction:

> *We estimate that the puzzle will require 35 years of continuous computation to solve, with the computer being replaced every year by the next fastest model available.*

In 2019, this challenge was shown to be quite a bit easier to solve, using either a desktop CPU or FPGA (in which case it took only two months of computation).

Although it was an interesting thought experiment of negligible practical interest, at least regarding the time-travel aspects, the initial paper suggested periods of months or years of computation.

Timing attack

An attack that takes advantage of timing differences to discover a secret and more generally compromise a cryptosystem's security. Sometimes, the running time of the algorithm depends on the value of secret inputs, which might trigger things, such as if–then patterns or some other variable-time operation. For example, some processors' arithmetic units will execute a multiplication instruction in fewer cycles if one of the inputs is zero. The textbook example of a timing attack targets square-and-multiply exponentiation (or double-and-add multiplication) where the private exponent (or scalar) is scanned bit per bit.

Attackers can also exploit timing leaks to identify the outcome of a cryptographic operation (such as padding validation) or the type of error that occurs when no detailed error code is returned (as with mitigations against Manger's attack).

TLS (Transport Layer Security)

A protocol to establish a secure channel over TCP (and over UDP with DTLS). TLS used PKI, X.509 certificates, and too many cipher suites until TLS 1.3.

🔒 See *SSL, Heartbleed.*

INDUSTRY CONCERNS

In September 2016, during the development of TLS 1.3, a representative of a financial services organization sent an email to the IETF working group in charge of TLS with the subject line *Industry Concerns about TLS 1.3.*

The message requested that TLS 1.3 consider integrating features allowing *supervised employee communications* (as mandated by some regulatory frameworks), or the capability to intercept encrypted communications under certain circumstances.

The chair of the working group, Kenny Paterson, responded:

Hi Andrew,

My view concerning your request: no.

Rationale: We're trying to build a more secure internet. Meta-level comment:

You're a bit late to the party. We're metaphorically speaking at the stage of emptying the ash trays and hunting for the not quite empty beer cans.

More exactly, we are at draft 15 and RSA key transport disappeared from the spec about a dozen drafts ago. I know the banking industry is usually a bit slow off the mark, but this takes the biscuit.

Cheers, Kenny

Tor

Of all cryptographic applications, Tor has one of the highest ratios between real-world impact and academic contribution and interest. The Tor anonymity network, also known as the *onion router*, provides untraceability guarantees if used correctly. Those for whom these are vital (criminals and law enforcement, as well as some journalists and political activists) use Tor to increase their life expectancy. You can also use Tor to bypass network restrictions (such as government censorship) and mitigate tracking and surveillance, which is why using it might get you in trouble in certain places.

Traitor tracing

Encryption schemes where different parties have a different decryption key to decrypt the same ciphertext. Traitor tracing aims, for example, to identify the source of a content leak and revoke access. But in practice, pirates can use a simple workaround: redistribute the content rather than the key. And anyway, large pay-TV deployments haven't really used purely cryptographic traitor tracing schemes.

Transfinite cryptography

Cryptography over transfinite numbers, that is, infinite numbers like $\aleph_0$ (the cardinal of countable sets, such as that of integers $\mathbb{N}$), $\mathfrak{c} = 2^{\aleph_0} = \beth_1$

(cardinality of the continuum, that is, of the set of real numbers $\mathbb{R}$), or $\aleph_1$ (the cardinality of Ω, the set of all countable ordinal numbers—itself an uncountable set).

Transfinite cryptography describes a computational model for working with such infinite numbers, as well as analogues of stream ciphers, block ciphers, and hash functions, and public-key signatures using said hash functions (via Lamport's construction).

An example of a definition is that of $\aleph_0$-one-way functions, which are functions computable in $\aleph_0$ operations and *practically impossible* to invert with *only* $\aleph_0$ operations. If such a function takes strings of length $\aleph_0$ as input, there are therefore $2^{\aleph_0}$ possible inputs, an uncountable number, preventing brute force even with infinite computational capabilities. Such a hash function isn't known to exist and intuitively sounds impossible to define.

Needless to say, transfinite cryptography can only be implemented in a Platonic universe of mathematical objects, not on your computer or on a future quantum computer.

Trapdoor

Not a backdoor. A trapdoor for some cryptographic function is a value, known to exist, that allows you to perform some operation that would otherwise be computationally hard. The best-known example is the RSA trapdoor permutation, which you can only invert using the RSA private key. A lesser-known example is that of trapdoor hash functions, such as VSH, for which collisions can only be found using the trapdoor.

Triple DES

Known as TDEA in NIST's official parlance. A cipher that consists not in three instances of DES but in one DES encryption, one DES decryption, and a second DES encryption. This is designed to emulate DES, because the Triple DES engine sets the same key for the first two instances, which then cancel themselves out. A Triple DES key can be up to $3 \times 64 = 192$ bits long. But Triple DES can't boast 192-bit security, because 1) each 64-bit DES key only has 56 bits of information, thus bounding Triple DES' security to 168 bits, and 2) meet-in-the-middle attacks can break Triple DES in approximately $2^{56 \times 2} = 2^{112}$ operations. Like DES, Triple

DES' security is also limited by its 64-bit block size. So, even though Triple DES still found in legacy applications isn't practically breakable, you've no reason to use it today. It fits best in crypto museums rather than modern applications. NIST retired Triple DES in 2018.

Trivium

A minimalistic hardware-oriented stream cipher that uses an 80-bit key. For several years, its circular representation was used on the banner of the DEFCON conference website.

True random number generator (TRNG)

🔒 See *Pseudorandom generator (PRNG)*.

Trusted third party

The solution to most cryptography problems. Sometimes a trusted third party is inevitable, and the cryptographers' job is to design protocols that minimize the level of trust required or that make any breach of trust detectable and recoverable.

Tweakable block cipher

A block cipher that takes an additional parameter, called the *tweak*, to ensure it produces different outputs with different tweaks. Unlike a key, a tweak isn't necessarily secret and usually changes more often than the key. Changing the value of a tweak should incur only a negligible performance penalty, unlike a key change, which usually involves a costly key schedule operation. Tweakable block ciphers have been used for disk encryption, for example, and for exotic proprietary constructions that need additional inputs.

Twitter

The location of the best and worst discussions about cryptography.

Twofish

AES candidate and finalist. Twofish is the little brother of Blowfish and has 128-bit-long blocks instead of 64-bit-long ones.

Quoting from the Twofish paper, Twofish's claims to fame included performance:

- Encrypt data at 285 clock cycles per block on a Pentium Pro, after a 12,700 clock-cycle key setup
- Encrypt data at 860 clock cycles per block on a Pentium Pro, after a 1,250 clock-cycle key setup

as well as cryptanalysis work:

> And finally, we cryptanalyzed Twofish. We cryptanalyzed and cryptana-
> lyzed and cryptanalyzed, right up to the morning of the submission dead-
> line. We're still cryptanalyzing; there's no stopping.

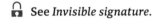

Undeniable signature

A signature that cannot be verified without the signer's cooperation, whether or not the signature is valid. Verifiers shouldn't be able to determine if a signature is valid without interacting with the signer, and the signer shouldn't be able to convince a prover that a valid signature is invalid, or vice versa.

🔒 See *Invisible signature.*

Universal composability

A theoretical framework for analyzing the security of combining cryptographic components, seeing as combining two secure protocols doesn't automatically result in a secure protocol. It's rarely applied to real use cases.

Universal hash function

A hash function used in cryptography that isn't the same as a crypto-graphic hash function. Unlike a general-purpose cryptographic hash, a universal hash function is parameterized by a secret key. Therefore, it's actually a family of functions, like a pseudorandom function.

But unlike a pseudorandom function, a universal hash function isn't pseudorandom in the cryptographic sense, only in the statistical sense: there exist no two input values M_1 and M_2 such that $\text{Hash}(M_1) = \text{Hash}(M_2)$ with abnormally high probability.

This property shouldn't be mistaken for collision resistance, however. Collisions are usually easy to find for universal hash functions.

Updatable encryption

An encryption scheme that can directly turn one ciphertext into another ciphertext, which can only be decrypted with a new, different key. A goal of updatable encryption is to perform key rotation on an untrusted system, as an alternative to the naive decrypt-encrypt approach.

Verifiable delay function (VDF)

A function whose computation cannot be sped up by extra parallelism or storage; therefore, it must be computed sequentially, like a proof of sequential work. But unlike the latter, VDFs admit only one solution.

🔒 See *Proof of sequential work, Time-lock puzzle.*

Verifiable random function (VRF)

The public-key counterpart of a pseudorandom function, where the public key can be used to verify that the output has been computed correctly by verifying the proof of correctness generated along with the function's output.

VRFs sound similar to public-key signatures but differ in two main aspects: a VRF's result is always deterministic (whereas a message can admit many valid ECDSA signatures, for example), and a VRF can generate a result and a proof (where the proof might be randomized).

VRFs have been used to build (theoretical versions of) lottery systems and transaction escrow schemes, and are used in several blockchain platforms.

Verifiable unpredictable function (VUF)

A function that somehow occupies a niche between signatures and VRFs: a VUF is like a VRF but isn't necessarily pseudorandom, only unpredictable. But unlike a signature, there must be only one valid output for a given message. A VUF scheme can thus be regarded as a unique signature.

🔒 See *Verifiable random function (VRF)*.

Vigenère cipher

A cipher more secure than Caesar's.

VSH (Very Smooth Hash)

A hash function with provable collision resistance, based on the hardness of factoring integers. But VSH (second) preimage resistance doesn't have as strong security guarantees.

Wallet

In cryptocurrencies, a set of accounts managed by a single individual or organization. Each account consists of a private key used for signing and an address somehow derived from the public key. Typically, these accounts are organized hierarchically, from one or more seeds, using BIP32 or a similar hierarchical derivation. This is convenient, because you can then manage a practically infinite number of accounts by storing only a single secret.

By extension, a wallet refers to any application or device that implements account management functionalities. Hardware wallets offer the best feeling of security, and sometimes they really are more secure. That said, they don't protect any better than software wallets against the most common risk: the lack of reliable backups.

Watermarking

The practice of embedding a value in some analog information (such as an image, video, or sound), usually during digital encoding, in such a way that the value can't be extracted or removed. In its most robust forms, it also survives noise, transcoding, and digital-analog-digital conversion.

White-box cryptography

Obfuscation at the algorithm level. Put otherwise, a means of implementing, say, AES in such a way that the implementation for a given key doesn't reveal the key. This sounds like magic, and like real magic, it doesn't actually exist, although advanced techniques give the illusion that it does. Most white-box techniques have indeed been broken, at least on paper. But in practice, they contribute to making reverse engineering harder, due to being supplemented by software-level defenses (such as software obfuscation, anti-tampering, anti-debugging, device binding, and so on).

Fundamentally, white-box cryptography is about transforming a symmetric cipher into an asymmetric one. If that were feasible, it would mean that we could create public-key encryption from a symmetric primitive, which would be surprising (despite the fact that we can construct public-key signatures from hash functions.)

Winternitz signature

An extension of Lamport hash-based signatures that can hash values greater than one. For example, to hash 4-bit messages, or integers between 0 and 15, you would publish $\text{Hash}^{16}(K)$ as a public key, and then sign a message $M \in [0, 15]$ by computing $\text{Hash}^M(K)$, where M is the number of hash iterations.

This works better than Lamport's binary scheme, but it still doesn't scale—just imagine the work involved in signing a 64-bit value.

WireGuard

A network-layer protocol for peer-to-peer secure channels that grew out of a kernel rootkit project. WireGuard was designed for SSH-like usage and VPN functionality. As per its creator's words, WireGuard is "cryptographically opinionated," which means it consists of a single suite of algorithms, as well as minimal cryptographic bureaucracy. Notably, it excludes certificates and thus ASN.1 or X.509 parsing. Unlike many projects, WireGuard has focused its efforts on cryptography and implementation quality with a much smaller code base than its alternatives.

Initially regarded with suspicion by the cryptographic intelligentsia, WireGuard's success and security track record now speak for themselves.

X25519

Diffie–Hellman with Curve25519.

🔒 See *Curve25519.*

X3DH

Extended triple Diffie–Hellman, a variant of Diffie–Hellman popularized by its use in the Signal protocol. X3DH combines multiple key pairs to compute one shared secret instead of using just one key pair per participant, as in basic Diffie–Hellman.

HOW X3DH WORKS

In its simplest setting, an X3DH operation between Alice and Bob works like this.

First, it combines their long-term identity keys IK_A and IK_B and their ephemeral, one-time keys EK_A and EK_B by computing the shared secret SK as follows, where DH() is a Diffie–Hellman operation:

$$DH_1 = DH(IK_A, EK_B)$$
$$DH_2 = DH(EK_A, IK_B)$$
$$DH_3 = DH(EK_A, EK_B)$$
$$SK = KDF(DH_1, DH_2, DH_3)$$

Here, KDF() is a key derivation function. Alice computes these operations using her private keys and Bob's public keys, whereas Bob does the opposite.

In practice, if Alice initiates the protocol, she'll pick a random ephemeral key and fetch a precomputed ephemeral key for Bob from the message server, where such keys are called pre-keys. X3DH was designed for use in asynchronous communications; it attempts to fulfill several security requirements in a way that minimizes computations and trust assumptions.

XMSS (eXtended Merkle Signature Scheme)

A public-key signature scheme that uses only a hash function and a tree structure. XMSS's statefulness—or obligation to keep track of a counter over signature operations—has been called *a huge foot-cannon*. Even so, XMSS has become an IETF standard and was experimentally integrated in OpenSSH.

🔒 See *SPHINCS*.

XOF (extendable output function)

A hash function whose output can be of variable size. The function can also extend the length of the output if needed. By contrast, in nonextendable, variable-size output functions, output values of different sizes are completely distinct, and the shorter ones aren't prefixes of the longer.

XOR

The exclusive OR logical operation, written as $\oplus$. XOR obeys the following rules: true XOR false equals true; true XOR true equals false; and false XOR false equal false. When viewed as a binary operator, the rules produce the following results: $1 \oplus 1 = 0 \oplus 0 = 0, 0 \oplus 1 = 1 \oplus 0 = 1$. Extended to bit strings, you'd get $0111 \oplus 1101 = 1010$, and so on.

XOR encryption

A straightforward form of encryption, sometimes used in malware as an obfuscation layer. It's similar to a one-time pad except that the XORed value isn't always secret or used only once.

Zerocash

Came after Zerocoin but before Zcash.

ZKP (zero-knowledge proof)

A protocol where a prover convinces a verifier that they know some mathematical statement (such as the solution to a hard problem) without revealing said statement.

Now a mainstream concept among crypto enthusiasts, ZKPs were once an obscure field at the intersection of cryptography and theoretical computer science.

Zero-knowledge is a broad and rich discipline, arguably still in its infancy as far as applications are concerned. There have been a few ZKPs advancing from conference proceedings to the real world: these applications include e-voting and blockchain applications, wherein non-interactive ZKPs help protect the privacy of transactions. ZKPs are also a component of threshold signing schemes as used for certain cold storage systems.

Cryptographic zero-knowledge shouldn't be confused with the security engineering concept of zero-knowledge architecture or with the marketing term zero-knowledge referring to client-side encryption.

🔒 See *NIZK (non-interactive zero-knowledge)*.

ZRTP

A key agreement procedure for RTP connections and used in voice-over-IP connections between two peers. Initially present in the Signal application to enable end-to-end encrypted calls, ZRTP was later discarded in favor of keys derived from the text messaging session state, which turned out to be simpler and more secure. The Z in ZRTP represents Phil Zimmermann.

INDEX OF TERMS

RESOURCES

Visit *https://nostarch.com/crypto-dictionary/* for errata and more information.

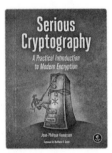

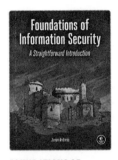

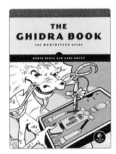